METHODS OF SOCIAL STUDY

Methods of Social Study

by Sidney and Beatrice Webb

---

with an introduction by
T. H. Marshall

Emeritus Professor of Sociology
University of London

London School of Economics and Political Science
Cambridge University Press

Published by the Syndics of the Cambridge University Press
The Pitt Building, Trumpington Street, Cambridge CB2 1RP
Bentley House, 200 Euston Road, London NW1 2DB
32 East 57th Street, New York, NY 10022, USA
296 Beaconsfield Parade, Middle Park, Melbourne 3206, Australia

Text of the 1932 edition,
copyright London School of Economics and Political Science
Introduction, © London School of
Economics and Political Science
This edition, © London School of
Economics and Political Science

ISBN: 0 521 20850 5

First published 1932
This edition 1975

Printed in Great Britain
at the University Printing House, Cambridge
(Euan Phillips, University Printer)

CONTENTS

Introduction to this edition by   *page* vii
   T. H. Marshall

Preface   xliii

CHAPTER I
The Province of Sociology Determined   1

CHAPTER II
The Mental Equipment of the Social Investigator   31

CHAPTER III
How to study Social Facts   54

CHAPTER IV
The Art of Note-taking   83

CHAPTER V
The Written Word   98

CHAPTER VI
The Spoken Word   130

CHAPTER VII
Royal Commissions and Committees of Enquiry as Sources for the Investigator   142

CHAPTER VIII
Watching the Institution at Work   158

CHAPTER IX
The Use of Statistics   202

CHAPTER X
Verification   218

CHAPTER XI
Publication   234

CHAPTER XII
The Relation of Science to the Purpose of Life   241

INDEX   261

INTRODUCTION TO THIS EDITION

T. H. MARSHALL

THE FIRST reference to *Methods of Social Study* occurs in Beatrice Webb's Diary on 18 March 1917. She was then recovering from a breakdown and wishing that she could retire to a quiet life in the country. 'Sidney meanwhile might complete those endless volumes of historical material which are almost finished, and the two of us together might write the two books we want to bring out before we die – *What is Socialism?* and *Methods of Investigation.*'[1] The 'endless volumes' were eventually completed, but not by Sidney alone – for Beatrice resumed her place in the partnership – and not until the end of 1928; it had been delayed because they had decided to bring the history of the Poor Law right up-to-date, and this had involved, not only much writing, but some new field-work. When, on New Year's Eve, they wrote the final words of the Epilogue of that great work, Beatrice declared that 'these two volumes will be the last big work of research'.[2] And so they were, apart from the unforeseen volume on Soviet Communism.

Nevertheless Beatrice found time, in 1921, to turn her mind to the projected book on methods and to prepare some draft chapters for it. These (or at least some of them) have been preserved among the Passfield Papers at the London School of Economics.[3] They were written in a personal style, using the first person singular instead of the familiar Webbian 'we', but they were based in large part on the summary statement about their methods of investigation which they had included in the Preface to their joint work, *Industrial Democracy*, published in 1897. Then Beatrice changed her mind. She was feeling moved to express in writing what she termed her philosophy of life by formulating 'on the one hand my faith in the scientific method as applied to social institutions, and on the other my realisation that, without the religious impulse directing the purpose of life, science is bankrupt'.[4] There is some evidence to suggest that she had tried to include the first part of this philosophy in her drafts for the book on methods. What we have of hers in the Passfield Papers starts with Chapter II, the opening sentence of which is: 'In the foregoing pages I have tried to explain the reason of my faith in a science of society.' But this sentence has been crossed out and the 'foregoing pages' are missing. In their place is a brief note in Sidney's hand-writing, beginning 'What we study is social structure', which lists topics for investigation and offers some precepts to investigators. Whatever the explanation of this, the fact remains that Beatrice decided, as she later expressed it, to 'cast on one side' the draft chapters she had written 'in order to put my experience of investigation into *My Apprenticeship* in an auto-biographical form'.[5] This was published in 1926, and she was still working on the second volume, which became *Our Partnership*, when she died.

So the book which 'the two of us together might write', was absorbed, for the time being, into 'this little book of my own – which is a big book in its high endeavour to explain my craft and my creed'.[6] But it reappeared in their immediate programme of work in June 1931, with its present title, *Methods of Social Study*. By that time, it seems, her interest in the project had somewhat diminished. Evidence drawn from her Diary has to be used with caution, as the entries sometimes express only a passing mood; but on this point they are frequent and consistent. In June 1931, she described the programme in which this book was an item as 'the plan for our dotage. I feel singularly light-hearted about it and regard it more as a way of keeping the old Webbs comfortably occupied than as an additional contribution to our output.'[7] When the time came to begin work, she gave Sidney the chapters she had written in the early twenties for him to use in 'preparing' the book.

In January 1932, she noted that 'he has added to and amended these chapters and is hard at work on the statistical method applied to social facts. Now I have to review what he has written.'[8] But she found it a struggle: 'My aged brain is so tired and strained that I find it difficult to grasp the task.'[9]

She was then 74 and advancing years were probably one of the causes of her very limited participation in the work, although it is true that she had made similar complaints more than once in the past, beginning as far back as 1917, and she proved able to cope with the visit to Russia and the two volumes devoted to it which still lay ahead. She also felt, no doubt, that she had already done her share of the work by writing the draft chapters, two of which (the crucial ones on note-taking and interviewing) she had published as Appendices to *My Apprenticeship*. In addition she was absorbed by a new interest. Russian Communism, which in 1926 the Webbs had regarded as being of the same species as Italian Fascism, had, by 1930, begun to look as if, in spite of its unacceptable features, it might contain the essential elements of the new social order for which they were looking – and she was reading everything she could lay her hands on about it. The entry in her Diary for 1 March 1932, sums up the story: 'S.W. with a little help from me, has finished the book on *Methods of Social Study*, whilst I have been reading

Lenin's works and various odds and ends on Russia.'[10]

It is important to assess Beatrice's share in the composition of this book because social investigation was very much her subject or, as she termed it, her 'craft' which, combined with her 'creed', had provided the inspiration for her professional, as distinct from her political, life. She had chosen the career of social investigator in her middle twenties, and had studied and practised the craft both on her own and also in close collaboration with Charles Booth. She had discussed with him, not only the methods of enquiry, in the sense of the techniques for assembling and handling data, but also its methodology, including the interplay of induction and deduction in the reasoning process. But though she regarded Booth as the boldest pioneer in the methodology of the social sciences, she did not find in him a warm response to her eagerness to press forward all the time with the creation of a science of society as the ever-present objective. Booth's idea was to build a statistical framework, not a theoretical structure, into which to fit the facts he discovered.[11] By the time Beatrice met Sidney she was the expert in social investigation, and he the novice. In 1891 she almost apologised for accepting his help in the study of trade unionism; the experience would be of value to him in his projected political career.[12] In 1919 *she* was helping *him* with the final chapters of the new edition of the *History of Trade Unionism*.[13] By that time Sidney had added his remarkable gifts to Beatrice's intelligence and acquired skills to produce the complete and balanced partnership whose methods are described in this book. Outstanding among his abilities were his astounding reading speed, the rapidity and fluency of his drafting, his photographic memory and his powerful, and above all orderly, mind. Mary Agnes Hamilton said of him: 'One glance at a printed page stamps its contents on the tables of his mind, and no accumulation produces either congestion or disorder there.'[14]

In the case of this book, however, the famous partnership did not function quite as it had done in its prime. Tawney once described it as 'one complex personality communing with itself', so that ideas 'were struck out in a continuous duologue in which each was flint and steel in turn'.[15] But this time there was little or no *continuous* duologue while the book was actually being written. The bulk of the material on methods was drawn from Beatrice's earlier writings, principally the draft chapters now in the Passfield Papers, *My Apprenticeship*, the Diaries (nearly the whole of Chapter VIII), and her article in the *Nineteenth Century* about the Royal Commission on Labour.[16] Sidney incorporated all this into the book with remarkable fidelity, expanding it considerably in places, but rarely altering the text – except that he replaced

the autobiographical 'I' by the Webbian 'We'
everywhere apart from the direct quotations
from the Diaries. Consequently the general
tone is more personal than in the other works
produced in partnership, and there are places
where Beatrice's more passionate temperament
has not been toned down as much as (she admits)
it generally was by Sidney's more down-to-earth
approach. Chapter VII, for example, reproduces,
not only the arguments, but also in places
the tone, of her savage, and rather reckless,
attack on the Labour Commission, which pro-
voked the Chairman, Sir Geoffrey Drage, to
reply with an article in which he said that
'anyone who has been present, as I have,
through the whole of the inquiry conducted by
the Labour Commissioners, and who knows the
facts, can hardly find the patience to read the
endless string of inaccuracies' in her account of
the proceedings.[17] There certainly were inaccuracies in it, but her case was fundamentally
sound and of vital importance. Royal Commissions did rely far too much on oral evidence, and
too little on verified facts.

In the chapters on methods, though there may
be some differences of style or tone, there is
complete unanimity of ideas and principles; in
the case of the first and last chapters of the book,
this is not equally true. At the beginning of the
Preface they say that the book as a whole is
about 'the methods of investigation' (its original,

1917, title) used by the Webbs themselves in their studies, but add that 'in our first chapter and in the last, we have attempted to define the scope and necessary limitations of the science of society' (p. xliii). The first sentence refers clearly to what Beatrice called her 'craft', and accurately describes the core of the book. The second refers, somewhat evasively, to the two halves of her 'creed' – faith in social science and belief in the importance to man and society of other values lying beyond the range of science. The final chapter does, in fact, expound the second half of her 'creed', using some of her own phrases in doing so. But only the last four pages are devoted to the subject. This section begins with a quotation from the Introduction to *My Apprenticeship*: 'Is man's capacity for scientific discovery the only faculty required for the reorganisation of society according to an ideal? Or do we need religion as well as science, emotional faith as well as intellectual curiosity?' (p. 255). The sentence that follows is an obvious echo of Beatrice's criticism of Herbert Spencer for trying 'to apply the scientific method to the *Purpose* as distinguished from the *Processes* of existence'.[18] But the treatment of this great issue is tame, and even at times apologetic; it reads very much more like Sidney (out of his element), than like Beatrice. The rest of the chapter offers some not very impressive examples of the beneficial effects of sociological research on social development, and describes some of the obstacles to planned social change and to accurate sociological prediction.

The first chapter is more substantial, but it steers clear of involvement in any theoretical discussion of the possibility of applying exact scientific methods to social data. Its centre-piece is an acceptable, but elementary, definition of sociology as the study of relations between people, their associations, and the structure and function of social institutions. This was, indeed, the basis of the subject as taught by Hobhouse and Ginsberg at the London School of Economics, but one would not gather from it that students there were also engaged in studying and discussing the theoretical issues raised in the works of Durkheim, Pareto, Max Weber and Marx. The chapter ends with a rather curious classification of institutions according to their origin in animal instinct, religion, humanism or deliberate planning, a classification which must surely have been invented by Sidney. It would seem, then (though we can only guess) that Chapter I as we have it is Sidney's substitute for the missing draft chapter, referred to in the cancelled sentence in the Passfield Papers, which Beatrice wrote to explain the reasons for her faith in a science of society. It must not be inferred that Sidney did not hope that such a science would be established. But, like Charles Booth, he thought it was as yet very much in its infancy, and he fought shy of philosophical argument about its nature. Beatrice tells us that he found much of her autobiography far too subjective, and 'all that part which deals with 'my creed' as distinguished from 'my craft' seems to him the sentimental scribblings of a woman, only interesting just because they are feminine'.[19] We might call this a fanciful description of a genuine difference between two intellectual temperaments, of which Sidney's was the stronger influence in their partnership. When, for instance, Beatrice stated emphatically in 1900 that 'our effort is now directed to one end – to establish on a firm basis a science of society', she was referring in the first instance to the foundation of the London School of Economics, and only in second place, and with many doubts and reservations, to her 'creed' and the possibility of fulfilling it through their own research work.[20] This might contribute some useful material, but the task itself must be entrusted to others, and to an institution which would outlast its individual members. Here she was undoubtedly voicing Sidney's opinion both about the role of their partnership and about the importance of the London School of Economics.

The basic principles of the Webb method of social investigation are: First, every statement made, whether by way of description, explanation, prediction or precept, must be based on facts. Second, the investigator must assemble and review *all* the facts in each case he studies. (This does not preclude sampling, where the cases in a particular class are very numerous. They used it themselves for parishes, and thought Charles Booth should have used it in his London survey.) Third, all facts and statements must be verified. Fourth, the investigator must be totally objective. He cannot (and should not try to) rid himself of bias, but he can, and he must, when at work 'put his bias out of gear'. These requirements are normal for any piece of empirical research, or would be so, if one were to insert the word 'relevant' before 'facts'. But this the Webbs were reluctant to do, and their discussion of the point is interesting and significant. It turns on the problem of how to start an investigation.

'The false start which pseudo-investigation usually takes', they write, 'is the plausible one of asking a question' (p. 34). Hypothesis on the other hand, is indispensible at all stages, 'and not least at the very beginning of the enquiry' (p. 60). Why so sharp a distinction between two things so closely related? For a hypothesis implies an antecedent question to which it offers a provisional and, if it is to serve its purpose, a testable answer. The explanation is that the kind of question the Webbs had in mind was one loaded with assumptions drawn from the investigator's personal prejudices or political ideals. They make this quite clear when they say that

the subject of study must not be 'a social
problem to which a solution has to be found, or
a question to which the investigator desires an
answer' (p. 56). For in such a situation the
investigator will unconsciously narrow the area
within which he looks for the answer. Hypotheses, on the contrary, enlarge the area of
search, provided you take as many as possible
into account, including, as they did, 'crazy ones,
plausible theories and fantastic ones, the dicta
of learned philosophers and those of "cranks"
and monomaniacs' (pp. 61–2). A question, in the
Webb's sense, imprisons an enquiry, whereas
hypotheses (in the plural) liberate it, by 'deliver-
ing the investigator from the strangle-hold of the
old categories of thought', as Beatrice expressed
it in her original draft chapter.[21] But hypotheses,
they realised, do more than this. They serve to
guide the investigator in his collection of facts,
and are 'one of the various handles by which the
students can, so to speak, take hold of the part
of the external world that is to be investigated'
(p. 61). They are invaluable, provided one is
always ready to change or to revise them. The
only 'right way' to enter on research in sociology
is to choose a particular social institution and
collect all possible information about it, 'with the
sole purpose of discovering every fact concerning
its constitution and its activities, together with
every ascertainable action and reaction between
it and its environment'. Out of this investigation

of the facts may emerge – in the end – 'the final hypothesis to which you apply your last test of verification' (pp. 41–3).

This problem of the relation between facts, questions and hypotheses provides a key to the understanding of the work of the Webbs, and in particular of this book about the methods they employed in it. They were operating in two fields which had to be kept apart (research and politics), and in two disciplines which had to be brought together (history and sociology). Tension was a possibility in both cases. On the first, Dame Margaret Cole has explained that they were engaged in 'labour research', which meant two things, both to them and to their colleagues. It meant 'research into subjects of importance to the Labour movement' and also 'research designed to establish conclusions in accordance with the general tenets of the Labour movement'.[22] Both used facts, the former for scientific ends, the latter (often on the same subject) for political purposes. Their determination to keep these two activities separate was perfectly genuine, and one of the main objects of this book was to show how this could be done and how, in fact, they managed to do it.

'Most orthodox historians', wrote Professor Postan in 1968, 'cling to the belief that their real business is to study facts.'[23] Sociologists, though they may also study facts, are particularly addicted to hypotheses. By these criteria

the Webbs fall into both categories. They des-
scribed what they called the 'Webb speciality' as
'a study, at once historical and analytic, of the
life-history of particular social institutions
during the last three or four centuries' (p. 89).
The words 'historical and analytic' cover the
two disciplines, but what follows shows a bias
towards history. And it was indeed through
history that they approached the study both
of trade unionism and of local government,
because they believed that, without a detailed
knowledge of its history, one could not hope to
understand the structure and function of a
social institution. Furthermore, their method,
based on a vast accumulation of facts, lent
itself to this approach, and also, as their work
demonstrated, to that kind of study of the
present which one may class as contemporary
history. It was, as they found, extremely
difficult (or even virtually impossible) to manipulate this mass of material (as a sociologist
would today, with the help of a computer) so as
to extract from it explanatory and theoretical, as
distinct from classificatory and descriptive,
results. What they in fact produced, in the main,
lay somewhere between straightforward historical narrative and full sociological analysis –
of the kind Beatrice, no doubt, had in mind
when, in 1886, she was 'puzzling over the
methodology of social science', and making up
her mind 'to try an article on social diagnosis'.[24]

On both points (the separation of science from politics and the passage from history to sociology) the story of their first two major works, *The History of Trade Unionism* and *Industrial Democracy*, is particularly illuminating. The former, generally acclaimed as an historical masterpiece, original and complete, seemed to them, according to Beatrice, 'little more than an historical introduction to the task we had set before us: the scientific analysis of the structure and function of British Trade Unions'.[25] So they started on the second book, in search of a thesis. But, 'when we come to the thesis we find the facts, tho' they can be used as illustrations, are not much good as the basis of our structure – they are only the ornament', and the argument turns out to be deductive.[26] In the same entry in her Diary she noted the tendency of the sociological element to develop political affiliations.

Our work suffers from being an almost unconscious attempt to unite three things: (1) a descriptive analysis of modern trade unions. . . ; (2) a criticism of trade unions (for the good of the unionists!); (3) an apology for, or defence of trade unions (for the enlightment of the middle-class and economists). These three objects do not amalgamate well.

These are, of course, only Beatrice's impressions, jotted down at the most trying moment in the passage from the first book to the second. But they identify correctly the issues they had to face, and the obstacles they had to overcome, or to circumvent. In *Industrial Democracy* they attempted to use the methods they had perfected in writing the history to produce an analysis of the contemporary scene which was sociological in the sense of being, not only descriptive, but also explanatory and, to a certain extent, theoretical. They never did this again. In the Preface to *The Consumers' Co-operative Movement* (1921) they say that it 'may be regarded as analogous to our *Industrial Democracy*'. This is true in so far as it is a contemporary, and not an historical, study. But there the analogy ends, for it is, as they rightly say, only a 'descriptive analysis', whereas the earlier work set out to be more than that.[27]

The book *Methods of Social Study* is presented to us in the Preface as offering a definition of the particular department of *sociology* studied by the Webbs and a description of the methods of investigation they employed in studying it. But all the chapters on method (Chapters II to X), except for Chapters VI and VIII (on *The Spoken Word* and *Watching the Institution at Work*) could be used, and were used by them, also in *historical* research. The main interest of the book to us today lies in the light it throws on how the Webbs worked and what their aims were; it is not a text-book for modern students, at least not in a technical sense; and (according to the Preface) it was not intended as such. But it clearly did have a didactic, and especially a cautionary, purpose. It is rich in common-sense

and frank in its account of the pitfalls which
that common-sense taught them to avoid and
out of which, when they had fallen in, it helped
them to climb. Their open-mindedness (that is
to say their receptiveness to the lessons of
experience) is remarkable, and their purpose
is to pass on the fruits of this experience to the
younger generation. The cautionary note is
strong in Chapter II where they list the qualities
needed for the daily tasks of social investigation,
which are often tedious and boring, and always
call for great patience and persistence. These
qualities, they add, are, in the England of today,
more often found in people with only a second-
class education (pp. 50–1). Did Beatrice remember that, shortly before she married Sidney, she
had written: 'we are both second-rate minds, but
we are curiously combined. I am the investigator
and he the executant?'[28] A nice example of the
quick response to experience is the advice to
the interviewer to remember that 'the mind of
the subordinate in any organisation will yield
richer veins of fact than the mind of the principal', not only because he is less on his guard,
but because he knows what is actually happening
(p. 137). This reflects what G. D. H. Cole called
her 'determination to study directly the practical
behaviour of persons and institutions'.[29]

The pivotal point on which their method
revolved was their system for the recording
and handling of the factual data on which all

their work was based. And central to this system
were the famous quarto sheets of paper, with
only one fact entered on each, docketed with
source and date and classified under a subject
heading. The solemn tone in which they wrote
(and spoke) about these pieces of paper has
given rise to some jokes at their expense, and
this has diverted attention from more significant
points about their method. There is nothing odd
about what we may call the 'unit-fact' method of
note-taking; it has been, and still is being, used
by many investigators, especially historians. In
both the earlier versions of the chapter on note-
taking (the draft in the Passfield Papers and the
Appendix to *My Apprenticeship*) Beatrice quoted
a passage from the *Introduction to the Study of
History* (1898) in which Charles Langlois and
Charles Seignobos state that 'everyone admits
nowadays that it is advisable to collect materials
on separate cards or slips of paper . . . furnished
with the precicest possible indication of origin'.
The detachability of these notes, they continue,
'enables us to group them at will in a host of
different combinations; if necessary to change
their places'.[30] This is exactly how the Webbs
describe and explain their own method, including the vital process of constantly 'shuffling'
the quarto sheets. So it is curious that the
relevant footnote in *Methods of Social Study*
(p. 84) should state that 'we have not found any
book informing the social investigator how to

handle his notes'. It is true that the French
authors, and also the German author cited by
them in the same footnote, were writing about
historical method; but the Webbs used their
similar method in both historical research and
social investigation.

Whatever others may have been doing at the
same time, it is clear that the Webbs invented,
or discovered, this method independently for
themselves. They started collecting facts for
their trade union history by means of a questionnaire, which they print in full in this book so
that the reader can see for himself why it was a
failure. It was, as they frankly admit, based on a
quite inadequate knowledge of the field. It was
too complicated, at many points inapplicable to
the situation it was investigating, and it begged
questions to which it was supposed to be seeking
answers. Rather surprisingly this experience led
them, not to try to improve their use of the
questionnaire as a technique of investigation,
but to abandon it altogether in their major
research. It could provide, they thought, raw
material for the statistician, but could not be
used for qualitative analysis (p. 75). For a time
they seem to have grouped their notes under the
source from which they were drawn, until their
assistant, F. W. Galton, switched to a system
of classification by topic. They at once saw the
benefit of this, but found that they could not
take full advantage of it until the notes had been

entered on separate sheets, so that those relevant
to each topic could be brought together in such
manner as the analysis of the material required;
and so the Webb method was born (p. 162 note).
Here, as elsewhere, they tackled their problems
in a kind of self-sufficient isolation. In her early
drafts for the book Beatrice wrote that she was
often asked what was the use of this elaborate
method of note-taking. 'Here I find myself driven
into an uncomfortable corner', she continued.
'Short of having as intimate a connection with
the work of other sociologists as I have had with
the Webb investigations. . . I am compelled to be
frequently taking these latter as proof of the
validity of the methods of research which I am
advocating.'[31] The same point is made on pp. 88 –
89 of this book, but in a much weakened form.

There is no doubt about the value of this
method; the question is to decide in what
circumstances and in what types of research it
can be profitably, or even safely, employed.
Nowhere as yet has the 'unit-fact' method of
note-taking been used on a grander scale, or
with more highly developed technical means of
sorting or 'shuffling' the data, than in the *Human
Relations Area Files* inaugurated by George P.
Murdoch in the 1940s to receive cultural data
about primitive societies. Yet even here some
anthropologists hold that the use which can be
made of factual information isolated in this way
from its context is limited, and that there is a

danger of it being misused through neglect of the qualitative differences between outwardly similar unit-facts. It is a question of the conceptual framework into which the facts can be fitted. As Clyde Kluckhohn put it, 'an altogether adequate organization of comparative data must await a better working-out of the theory of the universal categories of culture, both structural principles and content categories'. Present methods of organising and comparing data 'beg questions which are themselves at issue'.[32] The Webbs were, of course, working at a much lower level of generalisation and in a much more limited field, but they faced a similar problem, as the failure of their questionnaire showed. They hoped, by 'shuffling' and re-shuffling their data, eventually to discover the necessary principles and categories, even in the then uncharted seas of trade union history. Were their hopes justified?

When one browses among the boxes of original notes in the L.S.E. Library one finds it impossible to believe that these could really have been the source of their great works on trade unionism and local government. They are written by hand, in a variety of styles, and many are almost illegible. They range (especially in the early days) from brief items from a committee's minutes to literary extracts covering several quarto sheets. They are often classified under headings so broad that further sub-classification must surely have been necessary; but, as they gained in experience, the recording became more systematic. In one respect their method differed from that recommended by Langlois and Seign-obos. Immediately after the passage quoted by Beatrice in her footnote they say that, if items are interesting from several points of view, 'it is sufficient to enter them several times over on different slips'. This obviously reduces the amount of 'shuffling' necessary, and they presumably thought this desirable, because, as they say, 'in virtue of their very detachability, the slips or loose leaves are liable to go astray'.[33] The Webbs do not appear to have duplicated their notes and, considering the vast scale of their operations, and the relatively primitive methods available, this would hardly have been possible. So they had to rely on 'shuffling' and accept the risk of vagrant slips. Nevertheless there can be little doubt about the greatness of the books produced by these technically rudimentary methods. Their major works, said Tawney, 'stand out, amid the trivialities of their day and ours, like Roman masonry in a London suburb'.[34] While Clapham, reviewing *Statutory Authorities for Special Purposes*, said that their account 'can neither be summarized, because of its infinite variety, nor criticized, because of its complete originality'.[35] This is high praise from the two leading British economic historians of the day. How did the Webbs manage it?

One can imagine the method working satisfactorily where the subject-matter of the enquiry is clearly limited and the research is focused on some specific aspect of it. It could, as they themselves say, be used by ordinary intelligent and industrious people to produce monographs (see below, p. xxxi). What is so staggering about their own use of it is the scale of their operations and the immense volume of material which they were able to handle with what Tawney called 'new standards of comprehensiveness and precision'.[36] One must remember, however, that in their local government studies chronology, geography and the type of institution provided some easy bases for preliminary classification, so that they could, to some extent, deal with one thing at a time. In the co-operative movement they had a fairly homogenous subject, but not so in trade unionism which was marked by sharp differences of structure, function and policy. It was hard enough to describe and classify these differences, and harder still to try to explain them, as they did in *Industrial Democracy*.

They did not, of course, rely solely on the 'shuffling' of 'unit-fact' notes on quarto sheets of paper. When they had completed a research operation, like the study of a series of documents or the observation of an institution at work, they would often make an immediate summary report on it, and they found these reports very useful when they were writing the book. Then

they had an index – a copious one, by all
accounts, but not very efficiently compiled. One
of the oddest features of this book is that it
contains no reference at all to the role of an index
in the handling of data, a striking omission.
We must then add the personal qualities of the
authors – Beatrice's dedication, energy and
endurance (in her younger years) and Sidney's
fabulous memory. Galton, their first research
assistant, said of their system of note-taking,
filing and retrieval that it 'worked quite satisfactorily on the whole, but could not have done
so without Webb's remarkable memory'.[37]
Nevertheless there can be little doubt that slips
did sometimes go astray, or get overlooked,
in the course of analysis by the 'shuffling' of
pieces of paper. But, with such an immense
volume of evidence to draw on, it is unlikely
that defects of this kind would have any significant effect upon the conclusions. What is quite
certain is that they took infinite pains to correct
errors when they discovered them and to
improve their analysis when they saw how
this could be done. On one occasion they decided
to re-sort all their data about the Parish, and
Beatrice wrote: 'I shall index the whole of the
material under the four new heads.'[38] which
must have been a formidable task. On another
occasion they made 'an uncomfortable discovery'
– they had failed to take account of some important sources of information. 'It is not too

late, though troublesome, to remedy it', wrote Beatrice. 'But I shudder at the thought of how bad our work was three years ago. We ought to have known better.'[39]

In the Preface to *Industrial Democracy*, after setting out the basic principles of their methods of investigation, the Webbs went on to speak of the uses to which they could be put.

By the pursuit of these methods of observation and verification, any intelligent, hard-working and conscientious students, or groups of students, applying themselves to definitely limited pieces of social organisation, will certainly produce monographs of scientific value. Whether they will be able to extract from their facts a new generalisation applicable to other facts – whether, that is to say, they will discover any new scientific laws – will depend on the possession of a somewhat rare combination of insight and inventiveness, with the capacity for prolonged and intense reasoning.[40]

The point they are making here is that both these products of the scientific method are of value, and that both are, in their different ways, scientific. But they themselves do not fit neatly into either category. Their 'sociology' was not of the kind that is directed to the discovery of new generalisations 'applicable to other facts', nor could one properly describe their works as the monographs of conscientious students.

In *Methods of Social Study*, written thirty-five years later, there is a similar passage, but with a significant difference. It comes (p. 41) just after they had insisted that the investigator must not start with a question, but by choo sing his subject and then collecting all the factual information about it that he can find. They go on:

> It is the experience of investigators that, except by sheer accident, it is in this way only that anything novel is discovered; and certainly it is in this way only that we can ascertain the causal sequences, or as we say, the 'laws', that underlie this particular manifestation of external nature.

in such a way as to predict, and perhaps influence, the future course of events. Here the laws which may be discovered do not relate to 'other facts' but are specific to the subject of the enquiry. The object is, not merely to describe, but to understand and to explain a particular social institution or phenomenon. In one of her doubting moods, in 1900, Beatrice wondered whether the research on which they were lavishing time and money in an extravagantly complete manner would turn out to be genuine science. 'Shall we have the intellectual grasp to rise superior to our material – or shall we be simply compilers and chroniclers?'[41] They could both, at times, be surprisingly modest in their claims, but they did not accept quite as humble a role as that.

The 'Webb speciality', it will be remembered (p. xx above) was a study 'both historical and analytic'. In the case of local government history, for example, their aim was to discover 'the recurrent uniformities in constitution and activities showing the main lines of development, together with all the varieties of structure and function arising in particular places, in particular decades, or within peculiar social environments' (p. 89). This is analysis based on the classification of factual data, and classification is the key process in their method. Thanks to the completeness of their records and the constant 'shuffling' of their notes, they could pursue it with both accuracy and flexibility. 'The work of classification', they say, 'which the enquirer is perpetually revising and remaking as his observations and discoveries extend, is, in itself, an instrument of investigation' (p. 59). It leads to the identification of types – of institution, action and interaction – and so to the discovery of concurrent relationships and even of causal sequences. Knowledge achieved in this way, they believed, was more firmly based than anything previously available, and could, without being translated into generalisations, theories or scientific laws, greatly increase our understanding of society, its structure and its problems. Their views on verification point to the same conclusion. It is so important to them that they devote a whole chapter to it. Here they point out that logicians, and writers like Graham Wallas, regard verification as the final stage of discovery, that of 'transforming a hypothetical generalisation into a demonstrated theory, or even a "law of nature". The more modest sociological investigator does not find himself talking about laws of nature, and he is cautious

even about making sweeping generalisations'
(pp. 218–9). There is a personal element in this
comment (some do one thing, some another) and
it recalls what Beatrice said of Graham Wallas
when he died, shortly after this book was
published. She spoke of 'his skill and industry in
weaving his observations into instructive and
stimulating but inconclusive social studies'.[42]
But there is also a second element, a reference to
the backward state of sociological science,
which precludes such generalisations. Verification is therefore essential, not just at the final
stage of study, but at all stages. They elaborate
the point at the end of the chapter, making it
clear that, in their view, the most valuable
contribution of sociology to human knowledge
consisted in a body of verified and classified
factual information.

Leonard Woolf, who knew the Webbs well and
admired their work, though perpetually amazed
by their 'absurdities', spoke of their 'curious
habit of open-minded dogmatism'. They had
marked out an area of study as their own. Outside that area they would listen to anything you
had to say. Inside it 'one realised that they were
so strongly convinced of the soundness of their
central beliefs that consideration of any fact or
argument conflicting with them was purely
formal, and that their combined brain was being
unconsciously used as a powerful instrument for
bypassing inconvenient truths'.[43] This may

sound like a very severe criticism of their methods of investigation, but a closer look will mitigate that judgement. It is true that the whole programme of their empirical studies derived from a set of 'central beliefs' which emerged before the partnership had even started its work and survived unchanged to the end. The research left them unscathed. They were concerned with the ideal structure of a socialist democracy. This was composed of controls exercised over the economy and the social order by the citizens as consumers – partly voluntary, through co-operative societies, and partly compulsory, through institutions of political democracy, especially local government – and of a system of trade unions to protect the interests of the citizens as producers. What it rejected was control of industry by the workers, through producers' co-operation – hence the clash with the Guild Socialists. Their whole plan of work was based on this conception of the co-operative commonwealth, taking each of the three components in turn.

But this research was not designed to test these central beliefs, but rather to acquire the knowledge needed to put them into practice. It operated at a different level, which we might call microsociological as compared with the macrosociological character of the overall picture. The procedure they advocated for research at this level was, as we saw, to choose a

particular social institution, 'sit down patiently
in front of it', and collect all possible information
about it. Herein lay both the strength and the
weakness of their method. It was strong because
it enabled them to manipulate their vast
accumulation of factual data; it was weak in that
it treated each subject in isolation and with little
direct reference to its relation to the whole of
which it was a part. This may explain why their
*Constitution for the Socialist Commonwealth of
Great Britain*, which was intended to show how
their central beliefs could be put into practice,
was the least influential of their major works. It
also explains why Leonard Woolf's critical
remarks about the inviolability of their central
beliefs do not imply that there was, in their
empirical research, any similar reluctance to
accept what the facts told them was the truth.
Here they were engaged in 'pure' research, and
they followed their own rules. The approved code
of conduct, says Margaret Cole, was a little
different in what she calls 'tendencious research'
on behalf of a thesis with political implications.
In such cases it was permissible to engineer a
favourable presentation of the facts, though not
to distort or suppress the inconvenient ones.[44]

To make a fair judgement of the efficacy of
their methods, and of their scrupulousness in the
use of them, one must look at the work done
when the partnership was in its prime. Later on
Sidney became too occupied with other things

to exercise to the full his remarkable talent for documentary research, and perhaps also to do his share of supervision of the assistants to whom they entrusted it. And, as she grew older, Beatrice's style of interviewing (when collecting material for the final chapter of the Poor Law history) tended to become almost as didactic as it was inquisitive. Nevertheless it was in their old age they showed that they were prepared to revise (slightly) even their central beliefs. Before they went to Russia they had convinced themselves that, apart from the 'religious order' of the Communist Party, the Soviet Constitution corresponded exactly to the Webb Constitution. 'There is no d—d nonsense about Guild Socialism!', wrote Beatrice triumphantly.[45] But when they got there they found they were mistaken, and frankly admitted that co-operative production, which they had always condemned 'at any rate within the framework of the capitalist system', could evidently be a success in a Communist one. This was something they had been 'interested to discover'.[46] A mild, but significant phrase. For they had always been interested above all in discovery, and it was as an instrument for discovery that their methods of investigation had been forged.

.   .   .

NOTES

For full titles, see Bibliography.

Abbreviations

P.P. VII.   Passfield Papers, Section VII, part 2, Group (xii).

P.P.D.   Passfield Papers, Diaries of Beatrice Webb – typescript copies. This source is cited only for passages not included in the published editions.

D.1.   Diaries of Beatrice Webb, 1912–24, 1952.

D.2.   Diaries of Beatrice Webb, 1924–32, 1956.

M.A.   My Apprenticeship, by Beatrice Webb, 2nd edn, 1946.

O.P.   Our Partnership, by Beatrice Webb, 1948.

1 D.1. p. 84. 18 March 1917.   2 D.2. p. 187. 4 Jan. 1929.
3 Section VII, part 2, Group (xii).
4 D.1. p. 218. 28 August 1921.   5 P.P.D. 13 Jan. 1932.
6 D.1. p. 227. 28 Oct. 1922.   7 D.2. p. 273. 19 June 1931.
8 P.P.D. 13 Jan. 1932.   9 P.P.D. 9 Feb. 1932.
10 P.P.D. 1 March 1932.   11 Simey, 1960, pp. 77–8.
12 O.P. p. 26, quoting Diary for 15 Sept. 1891.
13 D.1. p. 169, 18 Nov. 1919.   14 Hamilton, 1932, p. 26.
15 Tawney, 1953a, p. 126.   16 Mrs Sidney Webb, 1894.
17 Drage, 1894, p. 463.   18 M.A. p. 33.
19 D.2. p. 58, quoting Diary for 22 March 1925.
20 O.P. p. 168, quoting Diary for 22 May 1900. See also Beveridge, 1953, p. 395.   21 P.P. VII p. 47.
22 Margaret Cole, 1949, p. 148.   23 Postan, 1971, p. 48.
24 M.A. pp. 245, 247.   25 O.P. p. 43.
26 O.P. p. 45, quoting Diary for 10 August 1894.
27 S. and B. Webb, 1921, Preface, pp. v–vi.
28 M.A. p. 352, quoting Diary for 7 July 1891.
29 G. D. H. Cole, 1949, p. 281.   30 M.A. p. 364, footnote.
31 P.P. VII. p. 35.   32 Kluckhohn, 1953, p. 509.
33 Langlois and Seignobos, 1898, pp. 103–4.
34 Tawney, 1953c, p. 136.   35 Clapham, 1924, p. 290.
36 Tawney, 1953b, p. 3.   37 Galton, 1949, p. 32.
38 O.P. p. 178, quoting Diary for 8 Nov. 1904.
39 O.P. p. 179, quoting Diary for 15 March 1905.
40 S. and B. Webb, *Industrial Democracy*, 1920, Preface (1897), p. xxix.
41 O.P. p. 168, quoting Diary for 22 May 1900.

42 P.P.D. 9 August 1932.

43 Woolf, 1949, pp. 259–60. See also Woolf, 1964, pp. 114–19.

44 Margaret Cole, 1949, p. 148.　45 D.2. p. 298, 4 Jan. 1932.

46 S. and B. Webb, *Soviet Communism*, vol. I, p. 220.

BIBLIOGRAPHY

Containing all the works referred to in the Introduction together with a selection from those cited in the book itself.

Unpublished Sources

The *Passfield Papers* in the British Library of Political and Economic Science (London School of Economics), containing:

1 *The Diaries of Beatrice Webb* – a complete copy in typescript of the originals. A selection has been published in two volumes: see below.

2 *Section VII, part 2, Group (xii)* – a small collection of papers, evidently early drafts for the proposed book on *Methods of Investigation*, including one document in Sidney's handwriting and drafts in typescript, starting with 'Chapter 2', by Beatrice.

Published Sources

Beveridge, Lord (1953) *Power and Influence*, London; Hodder & Stoughton.

Booth, Charles (1892–7) *Life and Labour of the People in London*, London: Macmillan & Co. (Reprinted 1902–3).

Bowley, A. L. (1915) *The Nature and Purpose of the Measuring of Social Phenomena*, London: P. S. King & Son.

Clapham, J. H. (1924) Review of S. & B. Webb, 'Statutory Authorities for Special Purposes' in *English Historical Review*, Vol. 39.

Cohen, Morris (1931) *Reason and Nature: an essay on the meaning of scientific method*, London: Kegan Paul.

Cole, Dame Margaret I. (1949) 'Labour Research' in Margaret Cole (ed.), *The Webbs and their Work*.

Cole, Dame Margaret I. (ed.) (1949) *The Webbs and their Work*, London: Frederick Muller.

Cole, G. D. H. (1949) 'Beatrice Webb as an Economist' in Margaret Cole (ed.), *The Webbs and their Work*.

Cooley, C. H. (1912) *Social Organization: a study of the larger mind*. New York: Charles Scribner's Sons.

Drage, Sir Geoffrey (1894) 'Mrs Sidney Webb's Attack on the Labour Commission' in *Nineteenth Century*, vol. XXXVI, September 1894.

Galton, F. W. (1949) 'Investigating with the Webbs' in Margaret Cole (ed.), *The Webbs and their Work*.

Ginsberg, Morris (1934) *Sociology*, London: Home University Library.

Haldane, J. B. S. (1927) *Possible Worlds and other essays*, London: Chatto & Windus.

Hamilton, Mary Agnes (1932) *Sidney and Beatrice Webb: a Study in Contemporary Biography*, London: Sampson, Low, Marston & Co.

Hobhouse, L. T. (1924) *Social Development. Its Nature and Condition*, London: George Allen & Unwin.

Hobson, J. A. (1926) *Free-thought in the Social Sciences*, London: George Allen & Unwin.

Kluckhohn, Clyde (1953) 'Universal Categories of Culture' in *Anthropology Today: An Encyclopedic Inventory*, University of Chicago Press.

Langlois, Charles & Seignobos, Charles (1898) *Introduction to the Study of History*. Translated by G. G. Berry, London: Duckworth. The original French edition was of the same date.

MacIver, R. M. (1917) *Community: a Sociological Study*, London: Macmillan.

Muggeridge, Kitty & Adam, Ruth (1967) *Beatrice Webb, a Life 1858–1943*, London: Secker & Warburg.

Postan, M. M. (1971) *Fact and Relevance: Essays on Historical Method*, Cambridge University Press.

Potter, Beatrice (1891) *The Co-operative Movement in Great Britain*, London: George Allen & Unwin.

Rowntree, B. S. (1901) *Poverty: a Study of Town Life*, London: Macmillan.

Simey, T. S. & M. B. (1960) *Charles Booth, Social Scientist*, Oxford University Press.

Tawney, R. H. (1953a) 'Beatrice Webb 1853–1943' in *The Attack and other papers*, London: George Allen & Unwin.

(1953b) *The Webbs in Perspective*, The Webb Memorial Lecture, London: Athlone Press.

(1953c) 'The Webbs and their Work' in *The Attack* (as above).

Wallas, Graham (1926) *The Art of Thought*, London: Jonathan Cape.

Webb. *Note*: all the works by the Webbs, unless otherwise stated, were published by Longmans, London.

Webb, Beatrice *Beatrice Webb's Diaries 1912–1924*. Edited by Margaret Cole with an Introduction by Lord Beveridge, 1952.

Beatrice Webb's Diaries 1924–1932. Edited with an Introduction by Margaret Cole, 1956.

My Apprenticeship, first edition, 1926; second edition 1946.

Our Partnership. Edited by Barbara Drake and Margaret Cole, 1948.

Webb, Mrs Sidney (1894) 'The Failure of the Labour Commisssion' in *Nineteenth Century*, vol. xxxvi, July 1894. (The reference given on p. 143, note, of this book is incorrect.)

Webb, Sidney (1889) 'The Basis of Socialism, 2. Historic' in *Fabian Essays*.

Webb, Sidney & Beatrice (1894) *The History of Trade Unionism*. Revised Edition extended to 1920, 1920.

(1897) *Industrial Democracy*. Edition of 1920 with New Introduction (but original Preface), 1920.

(1921) *The Consumers' Co-operative Movement*.

(1926) *A Constitution for the Socialist Commonwealth of Great Britain*.

(1936) *Soviet Communism: a New Civilization?* 2 vols.

Wells, H. G. *et al.* (1931) *The Science of Life*, London: Cassell & Co.

Wolf, A. (1925) *Essentials of Scientific Method*, London: George Allen & Unwin.

Woolf, Leonard (1964) *Beginning Again. An Autobiography of the Years 1911–1918*, London: Hogarth Press.

(1949) 'Political Thought and the Webbs' in Margaret Cole (ed.), *The Webbs and their Work*.

PREFACE

In this short book we have done little more than give in detail the methods of investigation used by us in our successive studies of British Trade Unionism, Consumers' Co-operation, and Local Government. It is true that, in our first chapter and in the last, we have attempted to define the scope and necessary limitations of the science of society. But these pages do not claim to be anything of the nature of a treatise on methodology, or even on the place of social science or sociology in the classification of the sciences. They merely explain our own approach to an understanding of the department of sociology dealing with the upgrowth, the modification and the dwindling, sometimes even to insignificance—of particular kinds of social institutions. Hence the reader must not look for any discussion of the relation of political science to ethics, or whether or not there can usefully be a "pure" science of economics, proceeding by logical deduction from theoretical assumptions or postulates as to the universality or predominance of particular human motives—such, for instance, as the pecuniary self-interest of freely competing wealth producers, on the one hand, or, on the other, the class antagonisms of profit-making capitalists and proletarian wage-earners. Moreover, in the department on which our studies have been concentrated, we have been unable, through lack of qualification, to use, and perhaps even adequately to appreciate, the Statistical Method. Our speciality has been a comparative study of the working of particular social institutions in a single country, made by observation and analysis, through personal participation or watching the organisation at work, the taking of evidence from other persons, the scrutiny of all accessible documents, and the consultation of general literature. If students and investigators find the volume helpful, our aim will have been attained. Any of them wishing further explanations are invited to communicate with one or other of us.

SIDNEY AND BEATRICE WEBB.

PASSFIELD CORNER, LIPHOOK,
HANTS, ENGLAND,
September 1932.

CHAPTER I

THE PROVINCE OF SOCIOLOGY DETERMINED

IF this were a book on the methods of chemical study
it would not be necessary to begin with a chapter on
the province of the science of chemistry. But social
science or sociology [1] is neither so clearly marked off
as chemistry from other branches of knowledge, nor
is its scope so uniformly understood by all sorts and
conditions of men. A loose and indefinite impression
as to the exact sphere of social science may not interfere with our learning all that the citizen needs to
know about the constitution and functions of the
various social institutions amid which we live. If,
however, our object is to make new discoveries in
social science, that is, to extend in this sphere the
boundaries of knowledge—if, moreover, we desire to
make the best use of the instruments of investigation
and research that are open to us—it is important, at
the outset, to clear up our ideas as to the province of

[1] "The word sociology first appeared in print in its French form 'socio-
logie' in the fourth volume of Auguste Comte's *Positive Philosophy*, the
first edition of which was published in 1839. . . . Although the word
sociology is derived from both Latin and Greek, still it is fully justified,
by the absence in the Greek language of the most essential component."
(*Outlines of Sociology*, by Lester F. Ward, 1898, pp. 3, 4.)

1

the science on which our attention is to be concentrated.

Science, in any definition, means knowledge of the universe, or of some part of it. Those who apply themselves to social science or sociology seek knowledge about a particular part of the universe, that is to say, the various human groupings that we find existing all round the world. Human society, in fact, is made up of these groupings of men, from the family up to the nation, or even the world-wide League of Nations; from a college debating society up to the Roman Catholic Church; from the blacksmith fashioning the ironwork for the village up to the international steel cartel operating in conjunction with the loosely associated bankers of the world.[1]

Sociology accordingly belongs, like botany and zoology, physiology and psychology, to what may

---

[1] The facts relating to human groupings, it has been said, "fall into two great classes, (a) social relations proper—the actual interrelations of wills—and (b) social institutions, which are not actual interrelations of wills, but the determinate (and therefore willed) forms in accordance with which men enter into social relations. . . . Social relations are activities, the threads of life; social institutions form the loom on which the threads are woven into a cloth." (*Community: a Sociological Study*, by R. R. Maciver, 1917, p. 7.)

"Using this term in a broad sense, institutions embrace language, customs, governments, religions, industries, and ultimately art and literature." (*Outlines of Sociology*, by Lester F. Ward, 1898, p. 123.)

"We may define an institution as collective action in control, liberation and expansion of individual action. Collective action ranges all the way from unorganised custom to the many organised going concerns, such as the family, the corporation, the trade association, the trade union, the reserve system, the state. The principle common to them all is greater or less control, liberation and expansion of individual action by collective action." ("Institutional Economics", by John R. Commons, in *American Economic Review*, December 1931, p. 650.)

be termed the biological group of sciences, as distinguished from the group of physical sciences, which includes astronomy and mechanics, physics and chemistry. The distinction between these two groups of sciences is, as we shall see, all-important in the consideration of their several methods and their instruments of investigation, discovery, and verification.

THE SUBJECT-MATTER OF SOCIOLOGY

Like physiology and psychology, sociology has to do with human beings. But unlike physiology and psychology, sociology is concerned not with the individual man, regarded as a living organism having body and mind, but with the relations among men. These relations are manifested (as in vernacular speech and the family) in human society in its most primitive forms, and they extend to all its stages of development. Accordingly their study involves the observation of the behaviour of individual men in their innumerable varieties of association among themselves, including the study of anything else in so far as it has any part in the formation of human groups, or in their endless modifications.

We have said that the sociologist is concerned not only with the relations between men in association, and with the human groupings in which these relations are manifested, but also with everything that helps to create or modify those relations and groupings of men. These influential factors are manifold.

There are the influences upon each population of the physical geography amid which it lives; of the climate and the weather; of the fauna and flora; of the social heritage of race and language, religion and custom; of traditions as to history, national and local, and, by no means least in its effects, of both the past and the contemporaneous economic framework of the community. All this may be regarded as forming a sort of social atmosphere in which every man grows up, and in which, all unconscious of its weight, he lives and moves, and his contemporaneous social institutions have their being. Changing the metaphor, we may say that all these influences, contributing to make up the particular civilisation or "Kultur" [1] of each community, form, as it were, the matrix in which all its social institutions are embedded. Affecting all the institutions of each generation, this social matrix is itself perpetually influenced by them—the whole creating and maintaining a constantly changing *milieu* against which individuals may react and even rebel, but from the influence of which no one can escape.

Into this social atmosphere, with momentous and almost incalculable effects on the behaviour of men in their various groupings, we see entering successive waves of thoughts and feelings, which spread over entire communities, and, with increasing inter-communication, increasingly over the whole world.

---

[1] The German expression "Kultur" (which does not mean "culture", the German for which is Bildung) is best translated by "particular civilisation", not civilisation in general.

Outstanding examples of such waves are afforded by the great world religions, such as Buddhism, Christianity, and Islam. Further instances are the grandeur that was Greece and the glory that was Rome; and more than a thousand years later, the liberation of the spirit in what we know as the Renaissance and the Reformation. Sociologists do not always recognise that the stream of ideas disseminated to the ends of the earth by the past couple of centuries of scientific discovery, notably in physics and biology, represent influences on human society quite analogous to the foregoing. Even more important may be the lives of men of exceptional greatness whether in mental power or moral genius, in thought or in action, in literature or in war, which may even, quite unpredictably, overturn one society and create another. William James spoke of such men as social ferments, possibly exercising, without even being conscious of it, entirely disproportionate effects on the society of their time. For our present purpose it is needless to consider how far it is the idea, how far the emotion, and how far the power of personality.[1] All such influences, not in and for themselves, but only in so far as they create or modify social relations, or the institutions into which these relations are woven, fall necessarily within the province of sociology.

In one of his stimulating lectures at the London School of Economics, Sir Halford Mackinder, then its Director, summed up in a vivid way the spheres

[1] *Psychology and Politics*, by W. H. R. Rivers, 1923, pp. 51-2.

of the several sciences by an imaginative vision of the earth on which we live. To the astronomer the earth, with all that is in it or upon it, is only an "oblate spheroid" spinning in the void of space, merely one of the "heavenly bodies", all of which have to be studied in their shapes and sizes and "proper motions" and in their relations to one another. To other scientists the sphere of exploration is the earth's crust and all that is in it or upon it, so far as our means of knowing extend. Let us regard the earth as an onion, made up of a series of coats. Think away all except the solid crust itself (the lithosphere), and you have left the special subject-matter of geology (including geography, petrology, mineralogy, crystallography, etc.). Ignore the solid ground, and concentrate attention on the waters that envelop the earth (the hydrosphere), often penetrating far into the solid crust, and mixing upward with the air; this is the subject-matter of oceanography or hydraulics. But there is another envelope (the atmosphere), about which we are steadily acquiring knowledge; this envelope, intermixing with both earth and water, is the subject-matter of meteorology. Leave out of your mental vision both the solid crust and its two fluid envelopes, and fix your attention entirely on the swarms of living organisms that inhabit them (the biosphere); this is the subject-matter of biology, which may be divided, if desired, not only into bacteriology, botany, and zoology, but also into a fourth specialisation called psychology. We carry this vision two stages further than Sir Halford Mackinder needed for his purpose to do. There are yet other fields of exploration. Think away successively lithosphere, hydrosphere, atmosphere, and biosphere; and contemplate the network of waves or oscillations, or whatever they may be found to be, that give us the experiences of heat, light, magnetism, electricity, and radio-activity in the limitless medium that we used to postulate as the ether. This field of force surrounding our globe may seem too immaterial to be thought of, even by analogy, as a coat of the onion. But as a distinct part of the universe it falls to be studied as physics. And there is yet another envelope, no less immaterial than the sphere of physics, which presents to us phenomena different from those of the lithosphere, hydrosphere, atmosphere, and biosphere, and equally outside those studied by the physicist. Imagine only, as a sort of tenuous film, the web of patterns formed by the social organisations that exist all round the habitable globe. The supreme importance to ourselves of these social organisations, justifies, as we shall see, such a concentration of attention; whilst the immense variety and distinctive character of their attributes, disregarded alike by the biologist and by the psychologist, supplies, as every investigator discovers, an immeasurable field for exploration, in which the scientific world stands to-day only at the edge. This part of the universe, this particular coat of the onion—the web of social organisations, which we may visualise as surrounding the habitable globe, and for which, according to the latest fashion, the term "politsphere" [1] might be invented—is the province of social science or sociology. Particular departments or branches of this study, not always usefully dealt with separately, or wisely parcelled out, have been given special names, such as anthropology, history, linguistics or philology, jurisprudence, economics, political science, and ethics. [2]

There is another way of parcelling out the sciences, which may, if only by way of contrast, help us to fix the position that sociology occupies among its sister sciences. A favourite classification used to be one based upon the particular form of force to

[1] "Sociosphere" has been suggested by Professor J. A. Thomson (*The Control of Life*, 1921, p. 224.)

[2] We may recall the fact that, just sixty years ago, it was the ocean, the earth's watery envelope, the particular "coat of the onion" that we have termed the hydrosphere, that seemed, to the scientific world, the part of the universe that was least known, and at that time had been the least explored. In response to the appeal thus made, for the removal of the ignorance that was deemed a reproach to British science in particular (for did not Britannia rule the waves?), the British Government of the day authorised the equipment of the Challenger Expedition to explore with the utmost thoroughness the entire length and breadth and depth of the world's oceans and all that they contained—a huge investigation on which, from first to last, something like a million pounds was spent, with the gain of a great increase of the world's knowledge. (See *The Cruise of H.M.S. Challenger*, by W. J. J. Spry, 1878; *Report on the Scientific Results of the Voyage of H.M.S. Challenger*, by Sir C. W. Thompson, 42 vols., 1881–95.)

To-day, it might be suggested, the part of the universe which is least known to science, and which has been least explored, is the outermost envelope of all, the web of patterns constituting the social institutions of humanity. Unfortunately no appeal for the systematic exploration of this part of the universe is made by the scientists of this or any other country; and no government is sufficiently enlightened to equip an investigating expedition corresponding to that of H.M.S. *Challenger*. We are inclined to say that a millionaire might usefully set aside a quarter of his fortune for the organisation and execution of just such a complete and systematic exploration of the social institutions of the world, or of the English-speaking world, or at any rate of his own country.

which each of the sciences is devoted. We may begin
with the still mysterious attraction exercised by
matter upon matter—that is to say, gravitation,
which, in all its manifestations, and in relation to
all kinds of material objects, together with all other
forms of force causing the phenomenon of motion
among these masses, whether celestial (astronomy)
or terrestrial (mechanics). This is the subject-matter
of two of the world's oldest sciences. Or we may study,
not the relations between masses, but the relations
of the molecules (or perhaps it may be oscillations or
waves) among themselves—the great and ever-grow-
ing province of physics, whether our attention is concentrated on light, heat, magnetism, electricity, or
radio-activity. The province of physics seems to-day
to become steadily more closely connected with that
of chemistry, which is the study of chemical action,
or the phenomena manifested by the various substances, whether elements, compounds, or conglomerates, in their action and reaction on each other. All
the sciences in this group, whether astronomy or
mechanics, physics or chemistry, have much in common. They are alike essentially quantitative. They
are concerned with units of considerable stability
assumed to be identical one with another; units
which lend themselves to exact measurement, and
are therefore fully open to mathematical expression
and treatment.[1] Those who devote themselves to one

---

[1] This is the main line of cleavage made by Poincaré: "It is therefore
thanks to the approximate homogeneity of the matter studied by
physicists that mathematical physics came into existence. In the natural
sciences the following conditions are no longer to be found: homogeneity,

or all of these sciences are apt to think of them, and of their characteristics, as typical of everything that can be properly called science. But for many years even the most bigoted students of astronomy, mechanics, physics, and chemistry have admitted, as a science, the study that concerns itself with living organisms. These manifest one quite distinct characteristic—that of life—which, whether or not we regard it merely as a form of energy, and whether or not any intermediate forms may yet be discovered, clearly distinguishes this part of the universe from the spheres of astronomy or mechanics, physics or chemistry. The living organisms, though subject to gravitation, molecular activities, and chemical action, as are pieces of non-living matter, are yet, in the main, essentially different from non-living matter. "A living thing", as H. G. Wells reminds us, "moves about in response to an inner impulse . . . and not only does it move of itself, but it feeds . . . metabolism and spontaneous movement are the primary characteristics of living things . . . [they] display an impulse to reproduce themselves".[1] The units are not absolutely identical one with another, even within the same species; nor are they stable or unchanging even for a day. They are accordingly, as organisms, scarcely capable of complete measurement. It may be thought, indeed, that they manifest

relative independence of remote parts, simplicity of the elementary fact; and that is why the student of natural science is compelled to have recourse to other modes of generalisation." (*Science and Hypothesis*, by H. Poincaré, 1905, p. 159.)

[1] *The Science of Life*, by H. G. Wells, 1931, p. 4.

differences which are not quantitative at all, but definitely qualitative. In at least one of these living organisms (the human being) we find characteristics that we sum up as self-consciousness, or what we call mind, which, though it can be apprehended directly by each individual in himself, can be so apprehended in himself alone, and because it is beyond our sight or hearing, smell or taste or touch, can be studied in other human beings only as manifested in their behaviour. This, which is regarded as the highest development of the human animal, constitutes the special province of psychology.

At this point, in the classification of the sciences, or rather along this irregular frontier, we reach the province of sociology, because, as we have described, we have necessarily to include in it, along with the relations among men that are manifested in human groupings, also the factors—prominent among them being the thoughts and feelings of individual men— by which these human groupings are caused or modified. Do these thoughts and feelings fall within the province of psychology or that of sociology? Our answer is that they fall within the provinces of both these sciences, but in each case only to the extent to which they are connected with the remainder of the province of each.[1] The same may be said, indeed,

[1] "What is it on which our attention is focussed? If the nature of social structures, as created by and as fulfilling man's needs and purposes, then we are sociologists. If the nature of mind as revealed in the structures which they have built, then we are psychologists. It is a difference of attitude in regard to a common material." (*Community*, by R. M. Maciver, 1920, p. 65.)

as regards the relation between physics or chemistry on the one hand, and sociology on the other. In so far as physical or chemical discoveries influence human groupings, as they certainly do, they have necessarily to be studied, up to a certain point, by sociologists as well as by other scientists. There is, in fact, no ground for suggesting that those who pursue any one course of scientific investigation should be excluded from the provinces in which others are specially interested.[1]

The manner in which the several sciences overlap along this frontier line may be made clear by considering a particular example. Suppose that we wish to investigate the organisation of public education in present-day civilisation. We must certainly include in our purview: (i.) the social machinery of schools and colleges; (ii.) the discoveries of the psychologists as to the child's mind; and (iii.) the socially potent "ferments" emanating from Locke, Rousseau, Pestalozzi, Herbert Spencer, and so on. We may organise our work in any one of three

---

[1] We may note here a different classification of the sciences, which depends on the assumption, as it seems to us, that sociology is not, and cannot be purely scientific in its nature. In this view all knowledge is divided between "Naturwissenschaft," comprising everything from astronomy to biology inclusive; and "Kulturwissenschaft," including theology, history, jurisprudence, philology, economics, ethics, etc. The one group is supposed to be "wertlos" and "sinnlos" (innocent of the conceptions of value or meaning), whilst the other is "wertvoll" and "sinnvoll" (dominated by these conceptions). See *Kulturwissenschaft und Naturwissenschaft*, by Heinrich Rickert (Tübingen, 1926); and compare *Gesammelte Aufsätze zur Wissenschaftslehre*, by Max Weber (Tübingen, 1922). We think that "wert" and "sinn" enter no more and no less into one department of our scientific knowledge of the universe than into another. For the place of "purpose," in connection with all human relations to any part of the universe, see Chapter XII.

separate ways. Some investigators would choose the biographical approach, writing an elaborate life of, say, Jean Jacques Rousseau; examining, along with his behaviour towards his contemporaries, even his most secret notes of never published thoughts, equally with the ideas with which he endowed the world, and their effect on society, including the school system. Others would prefer the approach by the evolution of ideas, constructing a history of published thoughts and feelings relating to education, at whatever date or by whomsoever promulgated, and tracing the various effects that they may be deemed to have had on the elementary and higher schooling of the world. Others, again, would choose to begin with the social institution itself—say, the school and university system of a particular country at a given date—which they can observe and analyse, and in which they can detect and evaluate the various influences exercised, not only by the published ideas of Rousseau and others, but also by the climate and the racial characteristics, the economic and political circumstances, and, in fact, the entire social *milieu* in which the educational system exists.

We do not need to decide between these three ways of planning what is plainly a sociological investigation. The three ways involve the study of partially differing fields of facts. Any way of enlarging the bounds of knowledge is entitled to respect: the supreme test is whether it is successful. Our own experience leads us to prefer the third way, namely, that of starting with an exhaustive examina-

tion of the structure and function of the social institution itself, and then tracing in it the effects of
all factors whatsoever, mental, physical, and social,
to which ever sister science these factors may pre-
dominatingly belong.[1]

We have dealt at some length with the position
that social science or sociology holds in the classification of the sciences, partly because it is useful to the
social investigator to remove any ambiguity or

[1] There may be some among our readers conscious of a vague feeling
that we have not explicitly dealt with a rival view of the scope and method,
not of sociology in particular but of our whole conception of the universe.

As we understand it, the claim has been made by Hegel, on the one
hand, and by the Marxist philosophers of to-day on the other, that it is
not by a purely objective analysis of the phenomena of the external
world, even with all possible aid from ratiocination, experiment, and
statistics, that any valid science can be constructed, whether of the
human mind (psychology) or of social groupings (sociology). Any valid
science, they seem to say, must be based on "the idea" immanent in the
universe, of which the phenomena are only manifestations which cannot
be accurately apprehended and are not fully comprehensible except when
regarded as emanating from "the idea" underlying and conditioning
the whole evolutionary process. We can only say, by way of excuse,
that we deliberately include, as within the purview of the sociologist,
everything that can be shown to influence in any way the coming into
existence, the activity or the modification of any human grouping.
Unfortunately, we do not ourselves know of the existence of any such
dynamic "idea" or "law of the being" determining logically what any
society must become, as we understand to be postulated by the Hegelians.
What seems to us a similar claim is made by the Marxist philosophers of
to-day on behalf of "the Materialist Conception of History", and the
"dialectic method". This appears to us to involve the assertion that there
is some transcendental idea, or type, or curve, or pattern, to which the
future evolution of the universe, or of human society, must necessarily
conform. If there is any such influence at work, it is naturally a fit subject
for objective study, along with the phenomena themselves. But we must
leave that study to those who have become aware of the existence of the
suggested dominating influence. To us, the "Materialist Conception of
History" is merely one hypothesis among many; one which appears to
describe some of the phenomena of social evolution—notably some
features and results of the industrial revolution of the past two centuries—but not others; and which, like all hypotheses, may be useful as
an instrument of investigation but acquires scientific value only in so

doubt about the province of the science to which his work is devoted; and partly because a precise conception of the relations between the sciences increases our understanding of each of them.[1] Yet it would be a mistake to make too much of the specific provinces of particular sciences, or of the boundaries between them. The groups or classes, the genera or species, into which, for our own convenience, we divide the world's phenomena cannot, even in our concepts when we make them as accurate as we know how, be precisely separated by sharp lines. But, as Whewell pointed out, "classes are not therefore left quite loose, without any certain standard or guide. The class is steadily fixed, though not precisely limited; it is given, though not circumscribed; it is determined, not by a boundary limit without, but by a central point within; not by what it strictly excludes, but by what it eminently includes; by an example, not by a precept; in short, instead of a definition we have a type for our direction. A type is an example of any class . . . which is considered as eminently possessing the character of the class.

far as it is verified by objective observation of the facts. In particular, we are not convinced that any stages have been discovered, through which all social institutions must necessarily pass. "The student", says Morris Cohen, "finds nothing that can be called scientific evidence for the actual or necessary existence of these stages. Social evolution through necessary stages is a mythology, not so picturesque as the old theologic mythologies, but equally effective in quenching the thirst for genuine knowledge." (*Reason and Nature*, by Morris Cohen, New York, 1931, p. 382.)

[1] The separation of sociology into various branches, such as anthropology and history, philology and jurisprudence, economics and political science, has, of course, a practical justification in the differences in the technique of study that the several branches require.

. . . The type must be connected by many affinities with most of the others of its group; it must be near the centre of the crowd, and not one of its stragglers."

There is, indeed, a real sense in which science is one, with the single task of knowing a universe in which the provinces and frontiers drawn by the human mind have no objective existence. The division of our studies into separate sciences is justified only by its convenience in concentrating our attention upon particular ranges of phenomena, and by its utility in helping us to form generalisations that we find to be valid descriptions of these phenomena. The very continuance of social science or sociology as a separate category of study—as, indeed, that of chemistry—will depend on the world's experience of the practical utility of such a parcelling out of knowledge at the particular stage of the world's history that we may have attained.

Moreover, the method of science—the intellectual procedure by means of which we increase our knowledge of the universe—may rightly be regarded as common to all the sciences, however they may be parcelled out and classified. "Scientific thinking, indeed," to quote L. T. Hobhouse, "is not distinguished from common sense by any peculiar assumptions, by any limitations of method, or by any restriction to one field of experience rather than another. It is distinguished, first, by its motive. It aims at the discovery of truth and at no other result. It is detached from emotional, personal, or practical objects. It is distinguished, secondly, by its continuity and ex-haustiveness of treatment. It is not content with isolated results, but conceives its subject as a connected whole and investigates all that it can find which has a bearing thereon. It is distinguished, thirdly, by the exactness which in all its results it seeks to attain. Detachment, continuity, and accuracy are the three marks of any science, and any study so marked is scientific, no matter what its subject may be."[1]

But whilst the intellectual method is one and the same throughout all the sciences, each science has its own peculiar instruments or tools with which to grapple with its particular subject-matter. Such are, in astronomy, the telescope and the photographic camera; in physics, the galvanometer and the atom-smashing fiery furnace of the gigantic electric arc; in chemistry, the blowpipe and the balance; and in biology, the microscope and the scalpel. Social science is debarred from the use of these particular instruments, but, as it is needless to say, it has its own, appropriate to the peculiar nature of its subject-matter, to which detailed attention will presently be given.

THE FACTS WITH WHICH SOCIOLOGY DEALS

Let us now consider more closely the nature of the phenomena within the province of sociology. These phenomena, as we have seen, are not matter, whether

[1] *Development and Purpose,* by L. T. Hobhouse, 1913, p. 122.

living or non-living, but the relations found to exist among human beings in their groupings. Such a relation can be known and described as such, irrespective of the human beings whom it concerns, though not without them. A social institution, it has been well said, "is a mature, specialised, and comparatively rigid part of the social structure. It is made up of persons, but not of whole persons: each one enters into it with a trained and specialised part of himself. ... A man is no man at all if he is merely a piece of an institution: he must stand also for human nature, for the instinctive, the plastic, and the ideal."[1]

Such an entity has attributes of its own that can be apprehended and enumerated; it produces effects, directly upon the behaviour of the men and women whom it embraces, and upon other social institutions, and indirectly, through these human beings, also upon their material environment. But each social institution is, as a whole, incorporeal or non-material—much in the same sense as a biological species is incorporeal or non-material—and can be seen or felt only in particular items which are in all cases only partial manifestations of itself. In its entirety it can neither be seen nor heard, neither tasted nor touched. If, for instance, a student from Mars

---

[1] *Social Organisation*, by C. H. Cooley, 1909, p. 319. "An institution is simply a definite and established phase of the public mind, not differing in its ultimate nature from public opinion though often seeming, on account of the permanence and the visible customs and symbols in which it is clothed, to have a somewhat distinct and independent existence." (*Ibid.*)

wished to apprehend the social institution that we call Parliament he might be invited to view the crowd of members orating and gesticulating in the House of Commons, and then be shown the smaller and more sedate group in the House of Lords. He might see the King opening a new session of Parliament, and presently witness the ceremony by which Bills passed by both Houses receive the Royal Assent and become Acts of Parliament. But all these spectacles together are not equivalent to the social institution that we call Parliament. They are only a series of partial and transient manifestations of it. Suppose a modern, and technically more efficient Guy Fawkes destroyed in one great explosion King, Lords, and Commons, laying the Parliament House in ruins and consuming in flames all the material paraphernalia of throne and bar, of wigs and robes, of woolsack and mace. The social institution itself would not thereby be destroyed, or even permanently affected. Within a few weeks the particular pattern would be again existing. A new King would have been immediately proclaimed; writs would have been issued for the election of new members of the House of Commons; the King would have sent his writ of summons to the male heir of each deceased peer of the United Kingdom; the surviving Irish and Scottish peers would have been called together as heretofore to elect such of their number as they desired to represent them in the House of Lords for life and for one Parliament respectively; and a new session of Parliament, as the direct successor of that which the twentieth century Guy Fawkes had so catastrophically terminated, would be opened by the new King, with all its old habits and traditions, and with paraphernalia and ceremonies exactly resembling those which had marked the preceding session.

To apprehend the British Parliament, with any approach to accuracy or completeness, requires vastly more than looking at the men and women, the buildings and the paraphernalia, in which it, for the moment, takes material form. Any adequate comprehension of it demands a study of its history and its functions, an understanding of its relations to other social institutions and to the public at large— a knowledge of its spirit as well as of its form. Of every other social institution in Great Britain or the United States, the same might be said. "The most established customs and institutions", sums up an American professor of sociology, "are only states of mind which find expression in customary action." [1]

Can we say that social institutions have an existence independent of the human beings who are concerned with them? This would be going too far. They are independent of particular men, but not of the human society of which they form part. "They have accordingly the sort of permanence that human

---

[1] *Sociology*, by E. L. Hayes, 1930, p. 31. "It is often said that the Pilgrims in the *Mayflower* brought over to these shores their English institutions. They did, but where did they bring them? Were they packed in a cedar chest? Were they stowed in the hold of the *Mayflower*? No, they were in the minds of the pilgrims." (*Ibid*, p. 396.)

society itself possesses. They may and usually do change as each society changes, and especially as the thoughts of men in each society change."[1] They are, of course, not eternal. They may, with changes in the thoughts of men, gradually fade away, as indeed, chattel slavery and witchcraft have in most countries faded away. They may be gradually supplemented by new patterns, eventually in replacement of those that are fading away. But compared with particular living organisms these immaterial and intangible entities are relatively indestructible; actually more permanent than many a biological species; some of them perhaps nearly as indestructible as the material atoms themselves.

CLASSIFICATION OF SOCIAL FACTS

The relations between men—the social institutions that we have to study—differ considerably in character. Some of them are manifested in groupings that are transient and accidental, as among the fellow-travellers on a journey, or among the men and women jostling each other in a street crowd, or queuing up at a railway booking-office. On the other hand, some of them, like vernacular speech, or the conception of law, endure over many generations of men and are so firmly fixed and so stable

---

[1] "We know what we are, but no people knows what it might become in two generations. . . . Prevalent states of mind do not change without cause. But given the cause, they can change beyond assignable limits." (*Ibid*, p. 31.)

as to appear to each generation actually as permanent as the universe itself. Some of these relations and the groupings to which they give rise are —or at least seem to those concerned to be—entirely optional and voluntary, like the most primitive human mating, or membership of a twentieth-century social club. Others, again, like the mother tongue, which no human being can avoid acquiring, or the machinery of government in the modern state, are as universal, as ubiquitous, and as unescapable as gravitation itself. It is these stable and durable relations, together with those that are universal or are obviously enforced, that we think of specially as social institutions. But all these relations among men associated in social groupings, whether transient and voluntary, or definitely woven into social institutions, may also be classified in another, and, as we think, a more significant way, according to their origins, that is to say, the manner in which they have arisen in human society, and to certain general characteristics dependent on such origins. We may distinguish among them four main types or classes, according as the institutions have arisen from, or have been moulded by (a) animal instinct; (b) religious emotion; (c) certain abstract principles as to right behaviour, which we may term humanistic; and (d) deliberate planning, whether empirical or scientific, being particular forms of social organisation devised in order to attain specific ends, for which class we use the term "technical".

SOCIAL INSTITUTIONS ARISING FROM ANIMAL INSTINCT

The first of these classes of social relations or institutions—in primitive society the predominant type, but traceable even in some of our most highly evolved institutions—includes those which may be assumed to have been derived from our ancestors among the higher vertebrates. We see, in fact, among some of the backboned animals, a slowly emerging supersession of part of their inflexible instinct by a new and more effective kind of mental capacity. Many vertebrates, other than man, habitually apply, to the difficulties with which they meet, the method of trial and error. They play, they tease, they fight, they defend each other, they imitate the actions of others, they seem even to meditate, showing a capacity for adapting their behaviour to their changing circumstances. In all this, in marked contrast with the ants and bees, and all other lower animals, they are transcending the instincts that they have inherited, by a steadily developing intelligence. Some of them begin to manifest inventiveness, to fear the unknown and the dark, to dislike being alone, and even to exhibit signs of self-consciousness. At some stage in the long evolution—there seems now to be general agreement in accepting as the mark of achievement the knowledge of how to make a fire or the acquisition of conventional language in place or in supplement of mere ejaculations—we class these animals as human beings. Primitive man accordingly starts off with a lesser inheritance of instincts than his forbears.[1] He is born less completely adapted, and is able to learn by degrees what to do as he grows up. The whole development of *homo sapiens*, and therefore of his social institutions, is one long replacing of animal instincts by feelings and thoughts, leading to an ever-greater elaboration of social relations.

Among the social institutions believed to be derived ultimately from animal instinct are such varied forms as the family with all the developments of blood relationship; the horde, the tribe, and the mob; territorial jurisdiction and sovereignty, with their derivatives of government and law; some would add the acquisitiveness manifested in the conception of property; and with this most of the economic relations dealt with by the abstract economies of the nineteenth century. It is perhaps more accurate to say that the animal kind of behaviour, whilst being typical of all the institutions of primitive man, is subconsciously present also in the relationships set up by the social institutions falling into the other classes. For, even

---

[1] The question of how much has been derived from our animal ancestry, and how much is to be ascribed to human discovery, cannot be said to be decided. "I am inclined to the view", wrote one of the ablest of American sociologists, "that man is not naturally a social being; that he has descended from an animal that was not even gregarious by instinct, and that *human society . . . is purely a product of his reason*, and arose by insensible degrees, *pari passu*, with the development of his brain. In other words, I regard human association as the result of the perceived advantage which it yields, and as coming into existence only in proportion as that advantage was perceived by the only faculty capable of perceiving it, the intellect." (*Outlines of Sociology*, by Lester F. Ward, 1898, pp. 90-91.)

if all human behaviour be at root animal, it is
worked up into different patterns according to the
presence, in the human beings concerned, of religious
emotion, humanistic theory, or the capacity for
applied science, or any combination of these.

SOCIAL INSTITUTIONS ARISING FROM RELIGIOUS EMOTION

The second class of social institutions includes
those arising from religious emotion. Early in the
evolution of human society man began to reflect on
the nature of things, whether seen in daylight or in
his dreams. He recognised in everything something
resembling that of which he was conscious in himself
—an aliveness, an active principle, a spirit or what
was eventually called a soul. He felt the emotion of
fear, not only of aggressive animals or fellow-men,
but even more of the unseen spirits of which the
world was full. Perhaps the feeling of awe is as
primitive as that of fear. This fear or this awe led
to all sorts of magic, and to the medicine man,
eventually to the king by divine right. There arose
also the emotion of wonder and adoration, leading
to worship; of love, leading to prayer and to the
merging of self in the spirit of love; of tradition and
holy writ, interpreted by prophets and priests, and
declared to be the will of God. All this culminated
in the great religions of historic time, Judaism and
Christianity, Buddhism and Islam, with ecclesiastical institutions and codes of conduct curbing,

or canalising, or sublimating man's animal instincts —consequences which had, for the societies in which they were manifested, considerable survival value.

SOCIAL INSTITUTIONS ARISING FROM HUMANISTIC IDEALS

We come now to our third class, namely, those arising from certain intellectual conceptions about the right behaviour of man in society. The characteristic feature of this class of social institutions is that the originators almost always confuse what is with what, in their judgment, ought to be. Hence we term this class "humanistic". The most famous of these political creeds is that embodied in the American Declaration of Independence in 1776. "We hold these truths to be self-evident: that all men are created equal; that they are endowed by their Creator with inalienable rights: that among these rights are life, liberty, and the pursuit of happiness; that to secure these rights governments are instituted among men deriving their just powers from the consent of the governed; that whenever any form of government becomes destructive of these ends, it is the right of the people to alter or abolish it, and to institute a new government, laying its foundation on such principles, and organising powers in such form as to them shall seem likely to effect their safety and happiness".

In a slightly different form the same metaphysical

conception was elaborated in the Declaration of the French National Assembly in 1789 as to the "Rights of Man". Whatever we may think of the truth or validity of this creed of 1776 and 1789—remembering the existence of chattel slavery, and its continuance in the United States down to 1864, together with the enormous inequalities in personal riches that have actually gone on increasing—no one can doubt its potency in moulding the political institutions of the modern world. A typical and no less amazing example of the overwhelming power of an intellectual dogma is the course of events in Soviet Russia from 1917 onwards. Here we see a stupendous refashioning of the social institutions of one-twelfth of the whole human race, spread over one-sixth part of the habitable globe, carried out according to the dogma of a German Jew of genius, Karl Marx. Whatever truth or validity there may be in the "Materialist Conception of History"—the hypothesis that political institutions are determined by economic conditions—and exactly why this "law" should lead to a supersession of the "Dictatorship of the Capitalist" by a "Dictatorship of the Proletariat ", we need not discuss here. But the establishment, for the first time in history, of a whole network of social institutions deliberately aiming at an equalitarian state in which all men will have really equal opportunities of life, liberty, and the pursuit of happiness, may well prove to be the most momentous of all the developments of social organisation.

Social Institutions arising from Deliberate Planning for Efficiency in carrying out Social Purposes

The fourth class of social institutions is on a different plane from any of the three hitherto described. In those three it is the desired end, whether the satisfaction of animal appetite, the fulfilment of religious emotion, or the carrying out of the humanistic creed, which is the decisive mark of the class. When we come to the most modern of social institutions, we find that they are, for the most part, of the nature of devices or expedients consciously and deliberately adopted for the purpose of carrying out with greater efficiency, in some particular spheres, predetermined general ideals or purposes, to the nature of which they are themselves indifferent. Thus the purpose falls into the background, and it is on the perfection of the machinery used that the mind of man is concentrated. Efficiency is the sole object, as it is the supreme test, of social institutions of this class, which may be employed in the service of any social ideal or general purpose whatsoever. The special characteristic of social institutions of this class, which may be termed the technical or scientific, is that they are devised and organised according to the teaching of applied science. We may cite as examples such humdrum expedients, seldom thought of as social institutions at all, as the audit of public accounts, or the introduction of Summer Time. These changes did not

arise out of animal instinct, nor from religious emotion, nor yet from any conception of the rights of
man. They were based on the observation of the
behaviour of men in particular circumstances, and
of the way in which habits are formed, with the
object of altering habitual behaviour so as to make
it correspond to some actual or imagined public
convenience. It is because these quite modern social
institutions were thus scientifically framed that they
have, within a relatively short time, wrought in the
lives of men changes positively greater in magnitude
than some of the most ancient customs, or than some
of the most dogmatic of creeds. To this class of
social institutions belong not only the devices that
the American capitalists call "Scientific Management" and the Five-Year Plan of Soviet Russia, but
also the codes and services in every civilised country
for public health and public education, for factory
regulation and the handling of traffic on our crowded
highways, as well as innumerable other arrange-
ments for the improvement of our machinery of
government. All these forms of social organisation
are put in operation to fulfil an ultimate purpose
which has been defined apart from their specific
functions. The technical devices themselves, each
one concerned only for its own particular efficiency
in action, are, indeed, consistent with any scale of
values in human society, or with any conception of
the relation of man to the universe.

This fourfold classification of social institutions,
for which we claim no higher value than that of

practical convenience in handling the subject, may be described as based on the mentality from which the institutions arose. It would be easy to imagine other systems of classification which might have their special uses. We might, for instance, classify institutions according to the nature of the function fulfilled in society, such as economic, political, legal, religious, etc. Some advantage might be found in ranging institutions according to the climates in which they flourished, or the economic circumstances out of which they arose. None of these classifications seems to us to have any bearing on the methods by which the subject can be best studied. They may, however, serve incidentally to illustrate both the extent and the variety of the phenomena which the other sciences disclaim all intention of studying, and admittedly leave to the sociologist to explore. How best to undertake this task will be the subject of the following chapters.

CHAPTER II

WHAT is the mental equipment, what is the ideal
state of mind, with which the student should start on
the exploration of any specific piece of social organisation? First, he must be able to focus his attention
on what he sees or hears or reads. Secondly, he must
be prepared to set himself deliberately and patiently
to ascertain all the accessible facts about the social
institution that he is studying; and not imagine that
he can, until he has mastered these facts, discover
the solution of any problem, or obtain any useful
answer to any general question that may have been
in his mind. Finally, he must realise that he is
biassed, and somehow or other he must manage to
discount this bias. We deal separately with these
three warnings.

THE NEED FOR TRAINED ATTENTION

The first indispensable factor in successful investigation or fruitful observation, and one which is often

overlooked, is an efficient attention. It is quite easy
to read books or to hear lectures without apprehend-
ing one half of what they contain—a carelessness
amounting almost to blindness or deafness. For instance, it is not every reader of books who can
correct proofs with even a low degree of efficiency,
even when he tries deliberately to do so, owing to
sheer inability to see the printer's errors that are
plainly before his eyes. Similarly, few of those who
listen to a lecture seem to "take in" more than a
small proportion of the statements made by the
lecturer, or even to absorb intelligently the points
that he has most strenuously endeavoured to drive
home. This common failure of attention is not due
merely to intellectual dullness or slowness. Many
intelligent and even quick-witted people make a like
failure owing to a sort of kink in their minds, which,
unless corrected by mental training, will always
destroy most of their efficiency as discoverers, and
even reduce enormously their capacity as learners.
"How is it possible", wrote Clutton-Brock in 1922,
"for people to read or hear that which has not been
said? They can do it only because they do not know
what attention is. They try to attend, but some isolated sentence strikes them and instead of listening
to the sentences that follow it, they proceed to build
upon it *some notion of their own* of what the writer
or speaker is trying to say; and *this notion is what
they attend to*, finding a confirmation of it in any
fragments which reach their minds afterwards. In
fact, they theorise instead of trying to experience;

and usually their theory is based on their own experience, not on the facts, so that, from all writing or speaking, *they get only what they have brought to it*, and this is not what the writer or speaker has said."

This failure to take in that to which we have not previously been accustomed occurs equally when we are not reading or listening to what other people tell us, but observing facts for ourselves. The investigator, like the pupil, can by practising improve his capacity of attention; and especially the power of continuous attention for long periods, in which such men as Newton and Edison and Einstein are said to have excelled. Such super-concentration implies genius. But the absence of adequate attention for the ordinary work of research may be due to sheer egotism. Indeed, most people, without being aware of it, would much rather retain their own conclusions than learn anything contrary to them. We all know the student who uses question-time not to extract from the lecturer fresh facts or new arguments, but to exhibit the workings of his own uninformed mind, frequently wandering somewhere well outside the subject-matter of the lecturer's discourse. To be a good listener you need genuinely to desire to hear what others have to say, rather than to utter what you have yourself to say. There is, in fact, a "moral" defect at the root of the failure of most beginners to achieve discoveries. They fail, it has been said, "because they set out to prove something rather than to arrive at the truth, whatever it may be. *They do not realise that a good half of most research work con-*

sists in an attempt to prove yourself wrong. Intellectual honesty is discouraged by politics, religion, and even courtesy. It is the hardest and most essential of the habits which the scientist, whether professional or amateur, must form." [1]

Until the would-be investigator has acquired this habit, he will never make discoveries. The successful investigator is he who is eager to have the conventional classification upset, and the orthodox categories transcended. He has in mind the axiom fathered on Heraclitus, "If ye expect not the unexpected ye shall not find truth". "The progress of science," it has been well said, "always depends upon our questioning the plausible, the respectably accepted, and the seemingly self-evident." [2] Far from ignoring an entirely unexpected fact, or some phenomenon inconsistent with accustomed definitions, he hails it with joy. It is to him a positive pleasure that things should be other than he had supposed them to be; and it is this occasional delight which makes the stir and thrill of the investigator's art.

THE FALSE START OF A QUESTION TO BE ANSWERED

And this brings us to a danger point at the very outset of social study. The false start which pseudo-investigation usually takes is the plausible one of asking a question. We are all apt to begin by re-

---

[1] *Possible Worlds,* by J. B. S. Haldane, 1927, p. 174.

[2] *Reason and Nature,* by Morris Cohen, New York, 1931, p. 348.

ferring to the arbitrament of "the facts" some question in which we happen to be particularly interested, a question which has all the appearance of strict impartiality, but which is almost invariably what the lawyers call a "leading question", if only because it is necessarily put in a phraseology involving a particular environment or set of conditions. Almost always we find, when we look back upon it after further experience, that the very terms in which the question was couched implied an answer of a particular kind, or at least excluded answers of some other kinds, about which we had not been thinking. It is no verbal quibble when the experienced scientist remarks that, if he knew precisely how to couch his question, he would already know a large proportion of the correct answer. At the very least, the mere condensation of our enquiry into a question, or into a group of questions, capable of receiving an immediate answer necessarily makes us concentrate attention upon just such conditions, or upon just such an environment, or upon just such factors, as were subconsciously in our minds when we asked the question. We are led to focus our vision, without in the least meaning to do so, upon those facts that we already know, or, worse still, upon such of those facts as accord with the bias which has made us frame the question in such a way. If we assume that for the question to be answered in this way or that involves the rightness or wrongness of a given social environment or institution, there is an almost irresistible temptation to collect, by way of answer to the question, facts illustrating the success of what is liked and the failure of what is disliked. This implies no deliberate falsification; indeed, not even any conscious selection or rejection of evidence. The life of social institutions, past and present, is so varied and complicated, the social tissue of which society is composed is simultaneously in so many different stages of growth or decay, that the investigator cannot help running up against apparently endless facts verifying almost every hypothesis and justifying almost every conclusion. It is a law of the mind that, other things being equal, those facts which seem to bear out his own preconceived view of things will make a deeper impression on the student than those which seem to tell in the opposite direction. We notice these facts much more easily than we see any others, and they remain more firmly in our memory. And this concentration of attention makes us blind to facts of a different order, the very existence of which has been unsuspected by us. It has been truly said that things are seen through our eyes, not by them.

This may be illustrated from personal experience. One of the authors, as the daughter of a successful business entrepreneur in Victorian England, and as the devoted pupil of Herbert Spencer, was, as a young girl, inevitably biassed in favour of freedom of competition and freedom of contract, and against any attempt to interfere with the perfect freedom of enterprise of the profit-making capitalist, whether by the state or by combinations of wage-earners.

Impelled by intellectual curiosity, and uneasy in conscience at being one of a small minority of wealthy and leisured persons in the midst of a community of workers obviously suffering from insufficiency and irregularity of livelihood, she was impelled to test by enquiry the validity of the economic creed in which she had been reared. She honestly wanted to know whether freedom of competition and freedom of contract, with a minimum of state and municipal activity, did or did not lead to the greatest possible production of wealth for the world, and, therefore, to the fullest subsistence for the whole aggregate of people that the world's conditions allowed. The relevant facts seemed to lie all around her. There were reports of directors and managers as to the ruinous effects of strikes; detailed complaints by foremen about short-sighted restrictions upon apprenticeship or limitations on output; innumerable articles in newspapers describing the mischievous effects of the excessive cost of production resulting from high rates and taxes spent on public services, or of the clumsy building byelaws and sanitary regulations of the local authorities, or of the foolish protective tariffs of the United States, or those then newly adopted by the German Empire. And were there not, on the other hand, the life-histories of vagrants and chronic paupers collected by the devoted workers of the Charity Organisation Society, not to mention the lurid account of the "National Workshops" of the Paris of 1848, to prove that any attempt to make up wages to anything like complete subsistence, or to give outdoor relief to the able-bodied unemployed, merely increased the total volume of pauperism, and actually augmented, in the aggregate, the misery that it was intended to relieve? For a time the results of this referendum to the arbitrament of facts—which were not recognised to be selected facts—seemed to provide an answer satisfactory to the unwary mind. The student was as convinced as when she started out that a system of free initiative and enterprise for the capitalist profit-maker and of the fear of starvation for the manual worker who might find himself unemployed brought about the largest possible wealth production for all concerned, and the best world then and there practicable for humanity as it was. The first shock to her complacency came when she discovered that contemporary leaders of the wage-earning class, together with academic socialists, were employing exactly the same referendum to the arbitrament of facts, and were going to much the same sources for their collection of evidence, and were indeed often citing the same instances, to demonstrate a diametrically opposite conclusion. Their question, though concerned with the same events during the same period, was a different one. The poverty-stricken descendants of the master craftsmen, domestic manufacturers, and peasant cultivators, together with their academic spokesmen, were bent on discovering whether their state of miserable subsistence and insecurity of livelihood was not the direct and inevitable outcome of the profit-making industry itself, through the divorce of the workers from the instruments of production and the subjection of men, women, and children to the competitive wage-system. The very growth and expansion of the capitalist system in England, which seemed, to those associated with that system, to prove its superiority to any possible alternative, had recently been used by Karl Marx, on the irrefutable evidence of Parliamentary blue-books, to demonstrate that this same freedom of enterprise for the profit-making capitalist was pushing the mass of the wage-earners into ever-increasing subjection and poverty. Each side was asking a question, not at all the same question on the two sides, and unconsciously collecting the facts —true facts—which supplied *the answer that the form of the particular question had invited.* On discussing these rival collections of facts with a scientific medical man, he remarked that, in his opinion, neither the individualist nor the socialist would get much further in discovering the laws underlying social institutions, unless both of them gave up asking what he called "loaded questions", and proceeded to study, in the minutest detail, the structure and function of the social institutions themselves, irrespective of whether or not this seemed likely to lead to any answer to what they wanted to know.

"Supposing all the medical men", he somewhat cynically remarked, "had been divided into two groups, one financially interested in the production of ice and the other in the running of hot baths;

and that each group, imagining itself to be advancing medical science, had started out to investigate the question whether cold or heat was the best remedy for disease, medical men might then have gone on collecting facts—quite true facts—of illnesses cured and lives saved by the application of ice, on the one hand, and on the other by immersion in heated air, steam, or water, or by subjection to electrically-produced radiant heat. But we should have learnt nothing accurately about the human body, the laws of health, or the causes of disease. Probably, tired of collecting endless series of facts, each series proving its predetermined conclusion, we should have taken to persecuting each other as heretics or blasphemers against the true faith." "If there is", he added, "such a science as sociology, give up asking questions in which you happen to be interested, or rather, reserve them until you have made yourself master of everything that can be discovered as to the structure and function of the social institution that you profess to be investigating. When you have got so far, ten to one your original question will seem to you a silly one, and, in the form in which you stated it, probably not one to which an intelligent answer could be given." To sum up, let the question to which you wish to find the answer do no more than suggest to you the particular social institution that you will study, *and study that completely*, irrespective of whether the knowledge of fact that you are gaining seems to bear upon your original question or not. This, in our experience, is the best way, and perhaps the only way, to avoid the danger of exaggerating the importance, or even misinterpreting the significance, of the first "promising" discoveries that you make, and of failing to recognise other factors against which you have, unconsciously, some prejudice.

An Objective Study of Facts

Hence the only right way in which to approach the subject-matter of sociology is not to focus the enquiry upon discovering the answer to some particular question in which you may be interested. On the contrary, you should choose a particular section of the social environment, or, more precisely, a particular social institution, and sit down patiently in front of it, exactly as if it were a form of energy or a kind of matter, the type-specimen of a plant or some species of animal, and go on working steadfastly to acquire all possible information about it, with the sole purpose of discovering every fact concerning its constitution and its activities, together with every ascertainable action and reaction between it and its environment. It is the experience of investigators that, except by sheer accident, it is in this way only that anything novel is discovered; and certainly it is in this way only that we can ascertain the causal sequences, or as we say, the "laws", that underlie this particular manifestation of external nature, in such a way as to enable us to predict what will happen to it, under given circumstances, in the future, and how we may possibly, by deliberate intervention, alter what would otherwise be the "course of nature". Incidentally, by concentrating your whole attention on the facts as they present themselves to your study, in contrast with the way people assumed or expected that you would find them, and by arousing your intellectual curiosity into the facts as facts, and by acquiring keenness for the most minute completion of your scrutiny and your analysis, however trivial and insignificant may seem each additional detail, you will, to the greatest possible extent, put your own bias out of gear. This does not entail giving up your emotional preference for a particular social environment, or for a particular social institution, over other environments or institutions. Quite the contrary. If your emotional preference survives your accurate ascertainment of all the facts, the very knowledge of the proven coexistences and sequences which this disinterested and, as we say, scientific observation of external nature may have revealed to you, will enable you, as a parent, a citizen, an official or a statesman, to intervene all the more successfully wherever intervention is practicable, and (according to your own ideals) desirable. Nor need you abandon the hope of eventually finding the answer to the question or group of questions which had, at the outset, specially interested you. Indeed, at the end of your investigations into the facts—though not at the beginning —you may well find the questions in which you were originally interested taking shape as the final hypothesis to which you apply your last test of verification. Moreover, throughout the whole course of your investigations these questions may properly be retained in your mind as tentative hypotheses, among other tentative hypotheses, merely as aids in the observation and classification of the facts, and as supplying the outlines of provisional explanations of the facts. Both the hypotheses and the classifications, and any other provisional explanations that occur to you, need to be consciously tested, as you proceed, by more deliberate observations, by more instructed reasoning, and eventually by actual verification. But you need much more in the way of hypotheses than your own interested questions will supply. For this purpose, indeed, the questions put by persons of opposite bias from your own, persons of different past experience and different education, will be equally useful with your own, or even more useful. It may be suggested—taking the example already given—that if the individualist enquirers in the last quarter of the nineteenth century had taken as their hypotheses the socialist questions, and the socialist enquirers had taken the individualist questions, their common investigation of the facts might have proved on both sides more fruitful than was actually the case! This is the reason why, in sociological enquiries, there is a positive advantage in "group work" over individual effort—provided, that is to say, the members of the group co-operate in studying the same subject-matter, accept similar methods of investigation, and adopt a common technique which will permit them to be continually sharing in each other's discoveries, testing each other's hypotheses, and criticising each other's tentative conclusions. The very diversity of education and experience, of subconscious beliefs and prejudices— in short, of the forms of the inevitable personal bias —will go far to safeguard from error any sincere and persevering group of investigators.

The Inevitable Presence of Bias

"Know thyself" is the maxim uniquely imperative on the investigator of social institutions. For the greatest obstacle to the advancement of knowledge —an obstacle blocking up the very gateway of the enquiry—is an obstacle in the mind of the student, the presence of bias. He must take it as certain that he will not approach his subject-matter with complete intellectual disinterestedness. Nor can such an inhuman detachment be asked of him. "They are in error", exclaims a learned German, "who require that an historian should comport himself as a man without religion, without a fatherland, without a family".[1] This peculiar "stop in the mind" of a social

[1] *Lehrbuch der historischen Method*, by Ernst Bernheim, p. 762. 5th edition, 1908. Bernheim quotes Ranke's dictum: "it would be quite impossible, amid all the struggles of power and amid all the ideas which the greatest decisions embody, to have no opinion upon them;" and continues, "And Chladenius said that an impartial description does not mean that anything can be described without some point of view. It is not to be required that he, in his narrative, should entirely divorce himself of the attitude of an interested person or of a stranger or of a friend, or of an enemy, or of a learned person or of an unlearned person; the very nature of the mind negatives such an abstraction and deprives the spectator of

investigator follows from the fact that he himself, with his personal, class, and racial interests, with his peculiar vices and virtues, with his beliefs and unbeliefs, forms an indissoluble part of human society, which is the very subject-matter of his science; a part which may any day be desirably or undesirably affected by the true or untrue conclusions arrived at by his and other peoples' investigations. The authors have had the advantage of knowing, in the past half century, either personally or through their books, most of those who have, in Great Britain, devoted themselves to this youngest of the sciences. There has been no one of them in whom bias could not be detected. This is specially noticeable among those who have attained to any position in the public eye. Hence, when we are told that a particular person has been appointed on a Royal Commission or Government Committee—or when the work of a particular historian is recommended for use in the schools—on the ground that he is or claims to be an "impartial person", we may rest assured that this means merely that the selector and the selected *agree in their bias*. They are often both so sodden with a particular type of social prejudice that, like the man who is blind drunk, they are unaware of it![1] It is needless to point out that the bias need not take the

the very conception of a spectator upon which all historical knowledge depends."

[1] How serious and all-pervading may be the bias of the social atmosphere will be seen in the careful study by Mr. J. A. Hobson in his *Free Thought in the Social Sciences*, 1926. This seems to be insufficiently appreciated by those who have discussed personal bias (compare *Wie studirt man Sozialwissenschaft*, by Josef Schumpeter, Munich, 1915, p. 20).

vulgar form of personal, class, or racial egotism. Self-protective bias arising from their own material interests will be easily detected by students who are honest with themselves. But they should be aware also of a subtler and more pervasive bias; they should be alive to the existence, perhaps in sub-consciousness, of a personal preference for a particular set of human values, or for what they hold to be a desirable state of mind in the individual or the community.[1] It may be that such an investigator will start open-eyed with regard to the particular part of society that he is investigating; yet his ultimate judgment, the way in which he states the facts, and his inferences from these facts, will be influenced, not necessarily by class or racial interests, but by his ideals of what should be. This emotional preference, this creative choice for one state of mind over another, may well be deemed not only inevitable but also desirable. But, like the mother's love for her child, which may be the very object of her existence, it must not be allowed to interfere with the use of the intellect in discovering the process by which alone the purpose, whether it be a good or an evil purpose, can be fulfilled. The practical suggestion is that we must, if we are to arrive at correct conclusions—that is, if we are to succeed in making "our order of thought" correspond with "the order of

[1] Do we ever succeed in going to a foreign country with a genuinely open mind? We may think that we do; but, on reflection, we may discover that we have unconsciously sought to discover in what respects the foreigner has adopted our own ideas and our own standards—instead of endeavouring to appreciate what exactly were his ideas and his standards.

things"—seek to choose methods of approaching the subject-matter and of conducting our investigations that will, for the time being, throw our bias out of gear.

The Need for Sympathetic Understanding

Here we touch on a possible obstacle to investigation and a hindrance to discovery which is the very opposite of personal bias, and for which due allowance is seldom made. It has been suggested that, at any rate in the sphere of psychology and in that of sociology, no one can adequately appreciate in other persons—perhaps no one can even recognise in them —feelings, emotions, or intellectual experiences which the investigator has not himself in some degree felt or endured. Can a seeing person ever understand what life means to one blind from birth? If the social investigator has never known what it is to be absolutely dependent for maintenance of himself and family on exiguous weekly wages, and to be then thrown, without resources, into chronic unemployment, how can he appreciate the effect upon the wage-earning class, and upon the social institutions that can be influenced by that class, of long-continued unrelieved mass unemployment? And, to put the issue more generally, can the investigator, coming from one social class, ever accurately analyse the dynamic force and the specific direction of the feelings of another social class?

It is clear that a sensitive mind and broad human

sympathies, coupled with width and variety of experience, form part of the equipment of the ideal investigator, as they do that of the greatest novelist or dramatist. We are told by Hazlitt, in his essay on "Shakespeare", that "The striking peculiarity of Shakespeare's mind was its generic quality, its power of communication with all other minds—so that it contained a universe of thought and feeling within itself, and had no one peculiar bias, or exclusive excellence, more than another. He was just like any other man, but that he was like all other men. He was the least of an egotist that it was possible to be. He was nothing in himself, but he was all that others were, or that they could become. He not only had in himself the germs of every faculty and feeling, but he could follow them by anticipation, intuitively, into all their conceivable ramifications, through every change of fortune or conflict of passion, or turn of thought. He had 'a mind reflecting ages past' and present: all the people that ever lived are there."[1] We think that this same generic quality was characteristic of Goethe's genius, and that it accounts for the immortality of his work. We cannot expect our social investigators to be Shakespeares or Goethes. We may, however, warn them of the specific hindrance, in their vocation, of imperfect sympathies. They can be on the watch for the commoner sorts of social blindness or deafness, which makes us fail to appreciate whatever we have

---

[1] *Lectures on the English Poets,* by William Hazlitt, p. 71. World's Classics Edition, 1924.

not ourselves known. They can remember to take precautions against omissions and inattentions. They can arrange to supplement their own investigations by those of persons having different temperaments or different experiences. Above all, they can always keep in mind that, not even for the sake of extirpating their own personal bias, must they for a moment lose their abiding sense of human fellowship.

PRELIMINARY EDUCATION

Is there any particular education that will fit the student to carry out from start to finish a big and complicated investigation? As soon as the public becomes aware of the importance of deciding policy on political and industrial activities upon the basis of a genuinely scientific knowledge of the structure and functions of society, this question will require to be answered.

The present authors cannot claim sufficient knowledge or experience of alternative methods of training the intellect and the character to be able to answer this question. What may be useful will be for them to indicate the kind of faculties that they have found to be required by the sociological investigator, and to add their own very loose observations as to the results of particular kinds of education and of social antecedents upon the amateur scientist.

First, let us note the distinction between the faculties required in the technique of social investigation presently to be described, and the intellectual qualities called for both in the initiation of the enquiry, and in the successful application—which has to be both scientifically productive and effectively rendered from a literary standpoint—of what is discovered. For the daily routine of social investigation—which we shall presently explain in detail as the art of note-taking, the methods of personal observation and the interview, the use of documents and literary sources, and the collection and manipulation of statistics—the predominant requirements are patience and persistence in work; precision in the use of words and figures; promptitude of decision in picking out new facts and ignoring what is only "common form"; a genuine satisfaction in continuing to progress along a previously determined course; above all, that particular form of intellectual curiosity that delights in unravelling complicated details irrespective of their immediate relevance to the main lines of the enquiry — the impulse in fact of Browning's "Grammarian". "All the scholars of any distinction have possessed the instincts of the collector and puzzle-solver", remark MM. Langlois and Seignobos. And last, but by no means least, there is the great advantage of a handwriting sufficiently neat and legible, to render the subsequent reading of the notes by yourself and other people an easy, or at least, a not too repellent task. Now, all these capacities seem to us to be within the reach of almost every intelligent person who has been properly educated. It is unfortunate that they seem more generally developed in the England of to-day in men and women who have enjoyed some such training as that of the elementary school teacher, or that of the newer types of professionals (such as the auditor and the actuary), or that of the second division clerk in the civil service, than in all but the ablest of those who have had the advantage of what is usually called the Public School and University education in the humanities. Whatever may be the particular accomplishments or graces of the successful graduate in Arts, especially when he comes from a well-to-do home, it is disappointing to record that such students are, when they leave the university, often lacking in certain characteristics required for the daily task of sociological investigation. So many of them have a high standard of leisure and holidays; an impatience with what they feel to be mere drudgery; an objection to the uncomfortable conditions of life that are often called for in the methods of personal observation and the interview; a distaste for the boredom involved in intimate association with uninteresting or positively disagreeable people; an attitude of aloofness from the life and labour of the ruck of men and women who constitute the very object of the study in question; and the usual craving for "quick returns", especially in the form of attractive generalisations with political or other topical applications—all characteristics which, for the purpose of sociological enquiry, need to be corrected if it is desired to start without a grave handicap in the race for the advancement of knowledge as distinguished from that for the popularisation of ideas. On the other hand the wide reading in philosophy and history; the personal intercourse with politicians and journalists that may have been enjoyed; the intimate contact with leading men of business and highly placed civil servants; foreign travel; and a working acquaintance with foreign languages, literature, and institutions will give such graduates a great advantage in the work of initiating and organising an enquiry and in the literary expression of its results, over those investigators who have had a more intensive and more narrowly specialised training; and especially over those who have had to begin their working lives whilst still non-adult. Moreover, the predominantly mathematical training obtained by some students, especially if this has included a real application to statistics, gives such graduates advantages of their own in the use of the statistical method, even if they find it necessary to learn that the mathematician is in danger of paying for the superiority of his instrument by a tendency to undervalue the qualitative estimate of his data, leading even to unsoundness in his logical inferences. To the impatience with whatever cannot be discovered in a comfortable study and quantitatively expressed in a formula or an equation we shall subsequently recur. How best to combine in the education of a single individual, the training which produces the most effective daily work of the sociological investigator with that which enables the investigation to be most skilfully chosen and initiated, and ensures the most fruitful presentation and application of the result, is a practical problem of which we can offer no solution.

CHAPTER III

How to Study Social Facts

THE investigator in sociology, as in biology or indeed any other science, finds himself face to face with a bewildering mass of facts. It is not merely that, as the saying is, he cannot see the forest for the trees. At the outset he cannot even distinguish the trees, so numerous and so confusingly diverse are they. It is only by an initial mental effort that he can perceive that any of them are trees. The sociological student has, for instance, grown up in a group of human beings consisting of parents, brothers, sisters, and other relations. Only by taking thought does he realise that the family is a social institution, indeed the oldest and most ubiquitous of social institutions. He has been to school, to college, to evening classes: he has now to appreciate that the educational system of his place and time is a mighty complex of social institutions. So also is the government of his village or parish, his city or county, his nation, and even the world-wide international organisation of nations as yet only very partially developed. The same may be said of the means by which individuals gain their livelihood and the community obtains its wealth production, whether fashioned on the capitalist or on the communist system or on any other. Then there are the organisations of recreation and games, religion and science, poetry and art, and, indeed, every sort of cultural relations among men.

From out of this mass of social organisation, past or present, the student has to choose some specific subject for his investigation. He may be moved in his choice by all sorts of motives; by some special interest in the subject or merely by its easy accessibility; by the desire to find solution of some social problem or a means of overcoming a particular difficulty; by the demand for an academic thesis or by sheer love of the sport of investigation. But whatever the object or the motive, the decision of the would-be investigator should, in our judgment, if the question is to be scientifically fruitful, always take the form of a choice of a particular social institution, or a fragment thereof, to be intensively studied, in its structure and functions, and under all its aspects. It may be the past and present organisation, economic or political, of a parish or a city,[1] or even a particular family; it may be a business establishment, whether factory or mine, bank or merchant firm; it may be a stock exchange or a financial clearing-house; it may be history and

---

[1] For a survey of sources in this case see *How to Write the History of a Parish*, by J. C. Cox, 1895.

effects of a particular endowment, or class of endowments; it may be a whole industry or a religious denomination, in one locality or in one country; it may be a trade union or an employers' association, a particular profession or other vocation; it may be the entire political organisation of a tribe, a nation, or a race, or only some fragment of it. Whatever it is, the subject-matter to be investigated should be some definite social institution in whole or in part —emphatically, for the reason already given, not a social problem to which a solution has to be found, or a question to which the investigator desires an answer. Only by making his initial decision in this form will the social investigator start, from the outset, even reasonably free from the bias to which every human being is prone.

It goes without saying that the student's choice of subject should be wisely limited by considerations of practicability. Let him, at least at the outset, be modest in the task he sets to himself. Let him take, to begin with, a relatively small piece of social organisation for the investigation of which he has special opportunities in the way of easy access to facts: his own village, a single family, one trade or profession, one department of government, a particular charity or a particular form of social service, a specific period of time or geographical location, or what not. However small the chosen fragment of organisation, the investigator will, whether or not his investigation leads actually to discoveries, at any rate find the whole universe gradually becoming clearer to his view. He will also learn, by trial and error, how to use, perfect, and supplement the methods of investigation discussed in this book.

CLASSIFICATION

First there is the mental process of classification. The external world is not quite such a hopeless chaos of unconnected happenings—not quite such "a big and buzzing confusion", to use an expression of William James—as a supernaturally precocious infant may be supposed to imagine at first sight. By the time he becomes adult even the most unreflective and least educated human being has picked up quite a lot of classification of experiences. As an investigator he must devise other categories or classes founded on or expressing particular attributes or particular relationships into which he tentatively fits the new facts that he acquires. We are warned that "no description of a large and varied mass of phenomena can be useful or intelligible without classification".[1] "No progress can be made" in sociology "without classification, *which is generalisation*".[2]

Every name or definition that is attached to what is observed is an assertion that the phenomenon is of a certain kind, and a tentative generalisation as to there being certain regularity in the external

---

[1] *History of Scientific Ideas*, by William Whewell, 3rd edition, 1858, vol. ii. p. 265.

[2] *Pure Sociology*, by Lester F. Ward, 1903, p. 53.

world. It is exactly the existence of such kinds and regularities that the investigator is out to discover.[1]

Another form of classification is presented by statistics, which necessarily relate to defined sets or classes of persons or events. The investigator should collect, at the outset, all the available statistics bearing on the subject of his enquiry; in order to include them in his sheets of notes, and retain them in his consciousness, if only as tentative classifications to be improved on.

The scientific investigator must, of course, be on his guard against taking any definition or classification or generalisation as to kind too seriously. None of these are anything more than words or sentences devised and disseminated by human beings according to such sensations and ideas as these particular people happened to have had in their minds. *They are not themselves the phenomena that they purport to describe.* The investigator must count them only as hints and suggestions for his work. "If anyone seeks", wrote Dr. Whewell, already in mid-Victorian times, "some ultimate and independent definition from which he can, by mere reasoning, deduce a series of conclusions, he seeks that which cannot be found. In the inductive sciences, *a definition does not form the basis of reasoning, but points out the course of investigation.* The definition must include words, and

[1] "The really important thing is to discover regularities, of whatever sort. Regularities make the world orderly, and a knowledge of them makes the world, or at least a part of it, intelligible and manageable." (*Essentials of Scientific Method*, by A. Wolf, 1925, p. 105.)

the meaning of those must be sought in the progress and results of *observations*." [1]

Our own experience has certainly confirmed Dr. Whewell's view. We described, in the Introduction to our first volume on *English Local Government*, how we had proceeded.

"During the first years of our researches into the actual working constitution of parish government, we almost despaired of constructing out of the varied and shifting relationships between church-wardens and constables, surveyors and overseers, the incumbent and the lord of the manor, the parish and the justices of the peace, any constitutional picture at once accurate and intelligible. But as we gradually unearthed from the archives the components of parish organisation in one district after another, as we observed the effect of different environments on the relations between these parts, and as we compared the results of our investigation in sparsely populated with those in densely crowded parishes, there emerged from our material a series of definite types, to one or other of which all additional instances seemed to approximate." [2]

This work of classification, which the enquirer is perpetually revising and remaking as his observations and discoveries extend, is, in itself, an instrument of investigation. Every new fact placed in a particular class either fortifies or weakens the im-

[1] *History of Scientific Ideas*, by William Whewell, 3rd edition, 1858, vol. ii. p. 198.
[2] *The Parish and the County*, 1906, p. 42.

plicit assertion as to attributes and relations that has been provisionally made by the creation of that class. Every class or category is, in fact, a tentative hypothesis as to co-existences or sequences, which has to be either completely verified, or else revised or disproved, by comparison with all the other relevant facts that can be discovered.

THE USE OF HYPOTHESIS

This brings us to the place of hypothesis in the scientific method. "An hypothesis", states Professor Wolf, "is any tentative supposition by the aid of which we endeavour to explain facts by discovering their orderliness". Our own experience is that, in the study of social institutions, on which alone we have any claim to speak, the hypothesis is a valuable instrument—indeed, an indispensable instrument—not merely at the last but at every stage of investigation, and not least at the very beginning of the enquiry. "So long as it can be put to the test, any hypothesis is better than none. Without the guidance of hypotheses we should not know what to observe, what to look for, or what experiments to make in order to discover order in nature. For observation not guided by ideas, even hypothetical ideas, is blind, just as ideas not tested by observation are empty." [1] Hypothesis is, indeed, not so much the triumphant outcome of prolonged investigation, on the point of being verified into a "law of nature", as one

[1] *Essentials of Scientific Method*, by A. Wolf, 1925, p. 23.

of the various handles by which the student can, so to speak, take hold of the part of the external world that is to be investigated. But only on one condition can this handle be safely used. The investigator must have in his mind, at any rate in all but the concluding stages of his work, not one hypothesis but many mutually inconsistent hypotheses. To start with a single hypothesis involves bias, which will hamper, if not prevent, the attainment of the very object of investigation, which is to discover new truth. The human mind is terribly apt to perceive what it looks for, and to be blind to what it is not looking for, especially where the emotions are concerned. For this reason, the investigator must specially beware of every kind of orthodoxy. The customary categories, in which the ordinary citizen is imprisoned, are exactly those from which the investigator must be perpetually trying to escape. He must therefore be always inventing new categories, and testing them on the facts as he perceives them—on the naked facts extracted from the customary categories with which they will almost certainly be clothed.

We have found it useful, in the early stages of an investigation, deliberately to "make a collection" of all the hypotheses we could at that stage imagine which seemed to have any relevance whatever to the special kind of social institution that we were dealing with. We noted them all down on our several sheets of paper, and others as we went along: wise suggestions and crazy ones, plausible theories and fantastic ones, the dicta of learned philosophers and those of "cranks" and monomaniacs, excluding only those that we thought had no possible relevance to our work, such as the prophecies extracted from the measurements of the Great Pyramid, or those of the astrologers. What we specialised on were, not the great hypotheses but such smaller ones as those about the way in which particular kinds of human beings of a particular race and period reacted to particular influences. And we never sorrowed over the discovery that our hypotheses proved to be faulty. We realised that, in the past, "many hypotheses which subsequently turn out to be false were fruitful all the same, because they suggested lines of investigation which, though they led to the repudiation of these hypotheses, also led to the discovery of truths".[1]

It is not easy to tell the enquirer how he can get together his collection of provisional hypotheses.[2]

---

[1] *Essentials of Scientific Method*, by A. Wolf, 1925, p. 23. The investigator who has had to abandon "one of his hypotheses should . . . rejoice for he (has) found an unexpected opportunity of discovery. Has the hypothesis thus rejected been sterile? Far from it. It may even be said to have rendered more service than a true hypothesis. Not only has it been the occasion of a decisive experiment, but if this experiment had been made by chance, without the hypothesis, nothing extraordinary would have been seen." (*Science and Hypothesis*, by H. Poincaré, 1905, pp. 150-1.)

[2] This stage of preliminary investigation, yielding a partial harvest of facts, but serving mainly for the collection of tentative classifications of the facts and provisional hypotheses about them, seems to spread over the four stages of Preparation, Incubation, Illumination, and Verification, in Professor Graham Wallas's account of the process. (*The Art of Thought*, 1926, ch. iv. pp. 79-107.)

The careless reader might believe that Professor Graham Wallas regarded them as more distinct and definitely successive than we have found them. But he clearly recognises their potential simultaneity. "In the daily stream of thought these four different stages constantly overlap each other

One way is to read at large about the subject-matter. The investigator who hopes to discover new truth, to extend, on some particular point, the area of the knowledge in the world's possession, must necessarily, at some stage in his work, familiarise himself with the area of that knowledge. He must necessarily push his way through to the very confines of the known before he can be sure that his finds are new discoveries. Thus, he must, at one or other stage of his work, acquaint himself with what has been published about his subject-matter. In this survey of the results of the work of his predecessors, he will incidentally pick up hypotheses. In our own experience it is here that subject-indexes of libraries, and subject-bibliographies, whether exhaustive or selective, are useful. At the very outset of the enquiry, a certain amount of time may usefully be spent in "browsing" about the subject-matter, not idly, but, at any rate, loosely; not merely looking through all the books about it, but doing so pencil in hand and jotting down all the ideas that occur to the mind. For this purpose, the "crankiest" pamphlets on the subject may be at least as fertile to the imaginative mind as the most authoritative treatises, the verified hypotheses of which may

as we explore different problems. An economist reading a blue-book, a psychologist watching an experiment, or a business man going through his letters, may at the same time be 'incubating' on a problem which he proposed to himself a few days ago, be accumulating knowledge in 'preparation' for a second problem, and be 'verifying' his conclusions on a third problem. Even in exploring the same problem, the mind may be unconsciously 'incubating' on one aspect of it while it is consciously employed in preparing for or verifying another aspect." (*Ibid*. pp. 81-2.)

possibly have exhausted their utility for discovery of new truth.[1]

On the other hand, one of the ablest of the American sociologists declared that it was his "observation that anything like an original view always comes gradually, and as a result of working through some sort of experience, rather than by the mere pondering of second-hand ideas".[2]

It is reported that when Newton was asked how he got the "ideas" (what we call the hypotheses) that he transformed into such epoch-making theories, he replied that it was by always thinking about the subject-matter itself—by keeping this constantly before his mind, and letting the faint dawnings of an idea open slowly, little by little, into a clear light. To put it another way, what is recommended is quiet,

---

[1] We add a footnote of experience:

"For many years", writes one of the authors, "I have made it a practice to begin my counsel to would-be researchers — indeed to everyone wishing to make any genuine investigation—by urging them to start by compiling a list of books, pamphlets and reports bearing on the chosen subject. The mere survey of their titles, publication and dates, and tables of contents is a necessary preliminary to every voyage of discovery after new truth. The second step is—not reading through these innumerable volumes, all of them more or less obsolescent, or at any rate of exhausted fertility—but skipping lightly over their pages, pencil in hand, to note down all the hints and hypotheses, cavilling objections, and irresponsible interrogations that will arise in the investigator's mind as he turns irreverently or even mockingly over the pages in which the craziest cranks have printed their fancies and venerable authorities have enshrined their standard doctrines. Then, and not till then, is the researcher in a position to begin his serious business of investigation; for the discovery of new truth without a whole assortment of hypotheses and pregnant observation of facts is difficult if not impossible. (*A London Bibliography of the Social Sciences*, by C. M. Headicar and C. Fuller, 1931, vol. i. Introduction by S. W. p. v.)

[2] *Sociological Theory and Sociological Research*, by C. H. Cooley, 1932, p. 7.

steady, continuous thinking at large about the subject-matter itself, uninterrupted and unharassed brooding; paying special attention, as Professor Graham Wallas suggests, to what dimly emerges "in the fringes of consciousness".[1] This is the way, it seems, in which Faraday got his fruitful hypotheses.

We conclude, with a distinguished English mathematician, that the emergence of new ideas or hypotheses "is not a strictly logical process, and does not proceed by syllogism. New ideas emerge dimly from nobody knows where, and become the material on which the mind operates, forging them gradually into consistent doctrine which can be welded on to existing domains of knowledge." [2]

"The way to get ideas", dogmatically summed up Samuel Butler, "is to study something of which one is fond, and to *note down whatever crosses one's mind in reference to it,* whether during study or relaxation. The worst way of getting hold of ideas is to go hunting expressly for them!"

The plain truth is that the investigator must, at this stage, give full play to his imagination, letting it seize on whatever it will. Later on in his investigation the imagination must, as Professor Haldane says, "work in harness", concentrating along the lines indicated by the observations of the facts that the investigator will be continually making. At the

---

[1] See especially chapters iii. and iv. of *The Art of Thought,* by Graham Wallas, 1926, pp. 59-107.

[2] *Science and Hypotheses,* by H. Poincaré, 1905, p. xviii of Introduction by Professor (Sir) J. Larmor.

earlier stages, "there is no reason", as Professor Haldane suggests, why imagination should not "play" with everything that occurs to the mind, especially in the dim light of the penumbra of consciousness, or on the fringes of full awareness, in order to collect hypotheses, "and it is perhaps only by so doing that one can realise the possibilities which research work opens up".[1]

Nevertheless, the investigator must hold all his hypotheses lightly, especially those to which he is emotionally attracted, even though these are just the ones that will seem to him the most useful. He must always have it present to his mind that these tentative categories and other hypotheses are not themselves truths, but only tools to be temporarily used in the discovery of truth. He must never let slip the fact that nature knows nothing of his hypotheses any more than of his categories or of his classifications, which are all only figments of the human mind, expressing or representing, not things as they are in themselves, about which man can know nothing, but only things as they appear to the mind of one rather exceptional person, with a single kind of education and experience, at one particular moment in time's eternity. Thus, the categories or classifications, in and through which we perceive, and as we fondly think, understand the external world, including what we call social institutions, must be assumed to change with every development of the human intellect. It is the very business of the

[1] *Possible Worlds*, by J. B. S. Haldane, 1927, Preface, p. vi.

investigator, in becoming a discoverer of new truth, to bring about an alteration of the categories and classifications which his predecessors, in the long evolution of man and his knowledge, have devised.

Not that we wish to deny that there may be some value in the firm holding of a fixed impression as to the most fruitful line of investigation to be pursued relentlessly in face of every discouragement. Some of Edison's inventions seem to have resulted from a seemingly unreasonable determination to try one substance after another until he found one that gave the desired result. Dr. Ehrlich tested no fewer than 605 separate drugs before discovering the remedy for syphilis which, after noting it merely as No. 606, he named salvarsan. Faraday's note-book records numerically, in the order in which they were tried, several thousands of experiments, many of them representing the untiring pursuit of apparently useless lines of investigation for which he had a fancy. That way lies infatuation (which is, after all, common to all who fall in love!); the very effective but dangerous social force of fanaticism; the *idée fixe*, and various recognised forms of insanity. It is hard to draw sharp lines of division between such affections of the mind. One practical maxim to the investigator is to beware of egotism, to be careful to check undue self-complacency, self-esteem, and *amour propre*. A useful expedient is intellectual discussion with the investigator's intellectual equals or superiors; and a deliberate open-mindedness to criticisms, even to the extent of forcing one's self both to feel and to express gratitude for the most destructive demolitions of one's own pet ideas.

THE MISUSE OF THE QUESTIONNAIRE

A record of misadventure is often of greater value to future explorers than a tale of unchecked advance. In our first investigation, that into the Trade Union Movement, we made a false start. What could be more promising than to open the campaign of investigation by elaborating a list of questions to be answered by those who knew the facts? We might thus, it seemed, avoid a sea of troubles—unnecessary journeys to and fro, and endless conversations with all sorts and conditions of men. So proud were we of these hundred and twenty questions, to which we had given a full week's work, displayed under twenty separate headings, on separate detachable sheets, with spaces left for the answers, that, without even estimating the cost, we forthwith ordered a thousand copies to be printed off. We visualised trade union officials sitting down to write detailed answers to these elaborate questions, whilst employers and government inspectors would turn over the leaves of our questionnaire, duly impressed with the impartiality and perspicacity of the Webbs, and convinced of the worthwhileness of correcting or supplementing their already extensive knowledge of the relations between employers and employed. Alas for the blank wall of self-complacency! Lest other students raise this particular barrier in their pathway to reality, we will explain, first, why our particular kind of questionnaire was foredoomed to failure; secondly, under what conditions and within what limitations a questionnaire may legitimately be sent out.

At this point the reader who happens to be also an assiduous apprentice in the craft of investigation will do well to study the questionnaire itself (printed at the end of this chapter), in order that he may the better follow our criticism. Regarded as a process of simultaneously pooling and reciting all the facts and hypotheses already in the minds of the little group of investigators, the drafting of these hundred and twenty statements, even in the equivocal guise of formulated interrogatories, had a distinct value. By this means we registered a particular stage in our enquiry, from which we could subsequently measure the extent and direction of our advance into the unknown. Further, these questions served as a useful memorandum, to be looked at before and after an interview, so that, in seeking new facts and following fresh clues, the familiar data and hypotheses about the structure and function of trade unionism should not be ignored in the interest aroused by new forms of organisation. For all these incidental purposes half a dozen manifolded copies would have sufficed. But for the originally intended object of automatically discovering facts unknown to us, either through the spoken or written word, the printed questionnaire proved a costly and even a pernicious failure. When we handed it to workmen or to employers, in the course of our interviews, their glum looks or stony silence, as they turned over the pages of this formidable printed document, convinced us, to put it politely, that the value of our pearls was not appreciated; and that any further display of them would actually injure our credit as sociological adventurers. When the copies were circulated by post, the result, with a few exceptions, was nil; either they found their way into the waste-paper basket, or they were returned with no more useful answers than "No", "Yes", "Partly so", "Sometimes one and sometimes the other", "Not applicable to this trade", or "Not possible to give instances". Exceptionally intelligent trade union officials, anxious to be helpful, ignored our question-naire and posted to us their current rules and annual report: a valuable result, but one which we could have obtained more easily and more universally if we had merely asked for these documents, without troubling the official with any questions. But this was not the whole of our mistake. The very know-ledge and skill that we had put into the questions, about which we were so complacent, proved to be our undoing. It was naïve of us to ask a trade union official to state in writing, concisely and yet ex-plicitly, whether the workshop committee exercised any control over the distribution of jobs, or over the conduct of the foreman; or under what circum-stances branches had refused or delayed to obey an executive ruling; or in what classes of jobs his craft had encroached upon or superseded others; or what subordinate and other workers, such as labourers and helpers, there were in the trade, but who were not admitted to the union. No one who did not combine the accuracy and zeal of a scientific worker with the trustfulness of a saint or a fool, could or would respond to any such inquisition into the working constitution and day-by-day activities of the organisation to which he belonged. Such information can be obtained, without much difficulty, but not in this way: not by a frontal attack all along the line, rousing suspicion, caution, and even resentment.

The inhibitory effect on the minds of the patients is, however, not the worst outcome of any such questionnaire. A more insidious evil is the paralysis induced in the mind of the operator. For the student of social institutions who approaches his subject-matter by way of formulated questions will find himself suffering from one or other kind of disablement. The slovenly habit, characteristic of distinguished personages on Royal Commissions and Government Committees of Enquiry, unaware of the complicated network into which they are intruding, of extracting answers to vague or abstract questions such as, "What in your opinion are the results of the legislative restriction of the hours of labour", leads to a sleepy satisfaction arising not from fullness of knowledge but from mere intellectual flatulence. But if, in order to avoid this dire complaint, the draftsman puts his interrogatory in precise terms, postulating the exact data that he requires, he will be, whether he recognises it or not, working in blinkers. The very form of his question will obstruct, if not entirely prevent, the perception of any fact not in his mind when he prepared his draft. "Do your members work at piece-work or at time-work rates" seems a fairly concrete question. But there are many other methods of remuneration besides payment according to the amount of the commodity produced, and payment according to the time spent in the service of the employer. As a matter of fact, there are so-called piecework rates which, on analysis, prove to be of the nature of time wages; whilst payments by the hour or the day not infrequently resolve themselves, in practice, into remuneration according to output. "How do branches take the votes of members: (*a*) by show of hands; (*b*) by circulars?" This question actually tended to conceal all other devices for ascertaining the wishes of the members. And the worst of it is, that the more exactly defined are the various methods of remuneration, or the more elaborately described are the various alternative ways of taking the votes, the more completely are excluded, from the answers elicited, any fact or sequence unknown to the investigator. Yet it is these very unknown co-existences and sequences that have to be discovered. If vague or general questions are asked, vague or general replies will be given. If, on the other hand, by the very form of the questions, categories and definitions are imposed, the deponent will confine himself within the limits of these stale facts and assumptions.[1]

Under what conditions and with what limitations can a questionnaire be used with advantage? It is not an instrument for use at the beginning of an enquiry. But, assuming that a whole range of occurrences have already been ascertained, and that what is needed is merely an enumeration of their location, either in space or in time, a precisely formulated questionnaire, confined to an enquiry as to where, when, and to what extent these facts prevail, and circulated broadcast among all concerned, may be the only practicable way of completing the investigation. Even in this case it is essential to have in view the probability of a sufficient proportion of accurate answers being forthcoming. For these reasons it is nearly always indispensable to limit the questions to those that can be answered by plain statements of such universally recognised facts as dates, numbers, ages, places, etc. The simplest and most obviously useful instance of a questionnaire, and also the one most extensive in its range, is the population census; and it is instructive to notice the limitations which have been found, by a century of experience, to be the conditions of its success. The date and place of birth or death, together with the age, sex, and marital condition of each person,

---

[1] This pitfall will not be entirely avoided by adding a general question to the specific ones. An enquiry as to which of two or three specified ways is taken will not be rendered harmless by merely adding a further question such as "What other ways, if any, are in use?" The very specification of particular ways fastens these upon the mind of the answerer.

are facts about which there is the maximum of universality and the minimum of ambiguity. When questions as to religion, occupation, or mental or physical defects are added, the success of the census questionnaire at once becomes doubtful; and it depends on the stage of popular education, and the definiteness of social structure as well as skill in drafting, together with the amount of personal assistance that can be given to the answerer, whether the answers to such enquiries are worth their cost and trouble. As an example of a successful private questionnaire, another of our investigations may be mentioned. When one of us was a member of the Poor Law Commission it became evident that, in some workhouses at least, the mortality among the infants born in them was excessive. It was important to ascertain how far this was common. Acting under skilled advice, we drafted a questionnaire not referring in any way to the rate of mortality. What was asked of each workhouse master was a list of the names of all the babies born in his workhouse during a precisely defined year, with the date of birth; if dead, the date of death; and if removed from the workhouse within the year, the date of removal. To prevent any suspicion of the real object of the enquiry the question was also asked whether each baby was legitimate or illegitimate. The actual particulars thus obtained revealed, neither to the workhouse master nor, even when aggregated, to ourselves, whether the infantile death-rate in any workhouse was greater or less than that among the population at large. But in the hands of an expert statistician, able to calculate not merely the proportion of deaths to births, but also the periods during which the several lives were "at risk", these answers, which the temporary authority of one of us as a Royal Commissioner enabled us (at our own expense) to make nearly universal throughout England and Wales, yielded a result which was as unquestionable as it was alarming. In short, a widely broadcast questionnaire is usually unavailable for anything more than the obtaining of the raw material of the statistician. It cannot be used for qualitative analysis. It may furnish confirmation of hypotheses, but it is very rare that it brings to light facts of structure or function not already within the knowledge of the investigator, or, at least, definitely suspected by him to exist. It is therefore not often useful in the discovery of wholly unsuspected truth.

NOTE TO CHAPTER III

AN ABORTIVE QUESTIONNAIRE

General

What is the full and exact title of your trade union, and the date of its establishment?

What localities does the union extend to?

What localities have the largest proportion of non-society workers?

What other unions are there in the same branch of trade—

    (*a*) Existing?

    (*b*) Extinct?

Has your union ever absorbed (by amalgamation or otherwise) any other union?

Federation

Is your union a member of any federation or joint committee of unions, and if so, which?

Are your branches usually members of the local trades councils, or of local joint committees with other unions?

Relation to other Trades

What other tradesmen compete most closely with your members?

Give any instance of overlapping, stating how settled.

Has there been any formal or informal decision as to apportionment of work with any other tradesmen?

Give any cases in which your trade has encroached upon or superseded others, and vice versa.

Membership

What is the total membership of your union—
  (a) Financial?
  (b) Non-Financial?

Give the corresponding total for the previous year or years?

State approximately the total number of workers in the United Kingdom in your branch of trade, distinguishing men and boys.

State exactly what classes or workers are admitted to your union; and in what proportion they stand to each other.

What subordinate or other workers, such as labourers, helpers, etc., are there in your branch of trade, who are not admitted to your union?

What proportion do such workers bear to those who are eligible for your union?

Is there any union of these workers (state name)?

Are such workers engaged and paid by your members, or by the employers?

Do they work at piece-work or time-work rates?

Are women anywhere employed on the same work as is usually done by your members?

If so, are such women admitted into your union? (State number of female members.)

What were the total receipts and total expenditure of your union last year?

What was the balance in hand?

Contributions

What is the present rate of contribution, distinguishing between the compulsory trade contribution and any optional addition for friendly or extra benefits?

Has this contribution varied since the formation of the society, and if so, when and how (state any changes as to compulsory or optional additions)?

If the union admits any members for trade benefits only, state the conditions of their admission, and how many there are?

What are the purposes for which levies have been raised?

Benefits

Have the number and amount of the benefits varied since the formation of the society; and if so, when and how?

Admission

Is any actual proof of indentured apprenticeship required, in practice, from a competent workman applying for admission?

Is any term of service specified as a condition of admission?

What provision exists for admission of competent workmen who have not served the legal time at the trade?

Describe any occasions on which the "books have been opened" to admit bodies of men not legally qualified.

Exclusion of Members

What is the practice as to the exclusion of members for non-payment of contributions?

What is the practice as to permitting excluded members to rejoin?

Executive

Of how many members does the Executive consist?

How often does the Executive meet?

Does its membership change much at each election?

Does it appoint sub-committees, and if so, for what purpose?

Does it, in practice, ever suggest to branches or districts to take action to obtain further trade privileges (such as higher wages, shorter hours, etc.)?

Delegate Meeting

What provision is there for calling a delegate meeting?

State the dates at which delegate meetings have been held since the formation of the society.

Does the delegate meeting consider any questions other than revision of rules?

Are the alterations of rules which are made by a delegate meeting submitted to vote of the members of the society?

Referendum

State the questions which have been referred to the vote of the members since the formation of the society (or within the last ten years).

Does the Executive itself submit alterations of rules or of benefits direct to the vote of the members, without a delegate meeting?

How are the votes of the members taken?

Are questions decided by a majority of branches, or by a majority of members of the society?

Give the subjects and numbers of some recent votes, so as to indicate the proportion of members who usually vote.

Appeals and Referee

Is there any appeal from a decision of the branch or district, and if so, to whom?

Upon what sort of questions are appeals usually made?

District Committees

Are the branches organised into districts, and if so, into what districts is the society divided?

How often in practice do the district committees meet?

Describe the kinds of business which are brought before a district committee.

How many branches are usually comprised in each district?

What is the usual attendance at a district committee meeting?

Are the branch officials usually members of the district committee?

Are all the branches organised into district committees?

Is there formal or informal organisation of district committees into local central district committees or otherwise?

Does the district committee ever take a vote of the members in the district; if so, on what subject and in what manner?

Are there any organisers, district delegates, investigators, agents, or other paid officials chosen by the whole society, but acting in or for particular localities?

Are all these officers appointed permanently, or for an occasion?

How are these officers appointed, and to whom are they responsible?

How many such officers are there, and at what dates were their posts created?

Do such officers in practice usually attend branch or district committee meetings?

Do they exercise any kind of inspection or supervision to see that the union rules are carried out?

If there is no such officers, who organises the district, and is in practice responsible for the carrying out of the T.U. regulations?

Branch

Is there rule or understanding limiting the minimum or maximum numbers in a branch?

What is the practice as to geographical limits of each branch?

How often, in practice, do the branch members meet for business?

Is any business done on the subscription night?

Describe the kinds of questions which are brought before the branch meeting.

What is the usual attendance at the branch business meeting?

Do the branches usually meet at public-houses?

If not, in what rooms?

Does the Executive experience any difficulty in exercising control over funds in hands of branches?

Give any instances in which branches have refused or delayed to obey the Executive ruling.

How do the branches take the votes of their members—

  (a) At meetings, by show of hands or ballot?

  (b) By circular?

Branch (Local)

State date of the establishment of the present branch of your union in this town.

Was there any previous branch in this town? If so, when and why did it lapse?

Is there any other union in this town which admits the same class of workers as your members?

Has your branch ever been an independent trade union? Or has it ever belonged to any other union than the present one?

Has it absorbed, by way of amalgamation or otherwise, any other branch of this or any other union; and if so, when and what?

Has there ever been any previous organisation in your branch of trade in this town; and if so, what was it called, and when and why did it lapse?

Is your branch a member of the local trades council, or any local joint committee in this town?

State the number of members—

(a) Financial;

(b) Non-Financial

in your branch now, and in previous year or years.

Has your branch any recognised working rules or standing orders? If so, kindly supply copy and state when obtained.

Has your branch ever before secured working rules in this town; if so, when and how were they lost?

Is there a recognised standard wage, and standard hours of work in your branch of trade in this town; and if so, what?

Do your members work piece-work, estimate work, or time work?

Workshop Committee

Does each shop or works select a committee or officers?

If so, what are the duties of this committee?

Is it responsible that the trade regulations are observed?

Do the members pay their contributions separately, or through the workshop committee or officers?

State occasions and subjects upon which the workshop committee and the branch have differed in opinion.

Does the workshop committee exercise any control over the distribution of jobs, or conduct of foreman?

Trade Regulations

Do trade regulations and standard wages differ from branch to branch?

Give the place and state particulars of the minimum and maximum "trade privileges" enforced by the union with regard to

(*a*) Hours;

(*b*) Wages;

(*c*) Method of remuneration.

What proportion of branches have their privileges formally embodied in bye-laws, working rules, standing orders, or other agreements?

What regulations exist as to the number of apprentices, and do these differ in different localities?

Do your members, in practice, refuse to work with non-unionists?

General

State any criticisms that are made upon the constitution or working of your society.

Can you suggest any improvement in it?

What Parliamentary legislation has been in the past advocated or supported by your society?

Are there any further changes in the law desired by your society?

Please supply any printed papers relating to your union that you can spare, such as reports, rules, bye-laws, circulars, lists of prices, etc.

Disputes

State dates and particulars of important disputes since the formation of the union, involving cessation of labour—

(*a*) General;

(*b*) Local;

(*c*) At individual works.

Will you state approximately the total number during the past year of disputes between your members and their employers, involving cessation of work, whether authorised or not?

State occasions and particulars when the executive has differed from branch or district respecting a dispute.

Is there any organisation of employers in your branch of trade—

   (*a*) National?

   (*b*) Local?

Does any system exist in your branch of trade providing for conciliation, arbitration, sliding scales, or other means of avoiding or arranging trade disputes?

CHAPTER IV

THE ART OF NOTE-TAKING

IT is hard to persuade the accomplished university graduate or even the successful practitioner in another science that an indispensable instrument in the technique of sociological enquiry—seeing that without it any of the methods of acquiring facts can seldom be used effectively—is a quite exceptional system of making notes, or what the French call *fiches*. For a highly elaborated and skilled process of "making notes", peculiar to this particular science, besides its obvious utility in recording observations which could otherwise be forgotten, is, in sociology, actually an instrument of discovery. This process serves a similar purpose in the study of social institutions, to the blow-pipe and the test-tube in chemistry, or the prism and the electroscope in physics. That is to say, it enables the scientific worker to break up his subject-matter, so as to isolate and examine at his leisure its various component parts, and to recombine the facts, when they have been thus released from all accustomed categories, in new and experimental groupings, in order to discover which co-existences and sequences of events have an invariable and therefore possibly a casual significance. To put it paradoxically, by exercising your reason on the separate facts displayed, in an appropriate way, on hundreds, perhaps thousands, of separate pieces of paper, you may discover which of a series of tentative hypotheses best explains the processes underlying the rise, growth, change, or decay of a given social institution, or the character of the actions and reactions of different elements of a given social environment. The truth of one of the hypotheses may, by significant correspondences and differences, be definitely proved; that is to say, it may be found to be the order of thought that most closely corresponds with the order of things.

The simplest and the most direct way of bringing home to the reader the truth of this dogmatic assertion of the scientific value, in sociological investigation, of note-taking, as an instrument of discovery, will be first to describe the technique, and then in greater detail to point out its uses.[1] Now, it may seem a trivial matter, but the first item in the recipe for scientific note-taking in sociology is that the student must be provided, not with a note-book of any sort or kind, but with an indefinite number of separate sheets of paper of identical shape and size (we have found large quarto the most convenient

[1] We have not found any book informing the social investigator how to handle his notes. A small French manual, *L'Art de Classer les Notes*, by Guyot-Daubés (Paris, 1891), deals principally with mechanical apparatus.

form), and of sufficiently good quality for either pen
or typewriter. The reason why detached sheets must
be employed, instead of any book, is, as will presently be demonstrated, the absolute necessity of
being able to rearrange the notes successively in
different orders; in fact, to be able to shuffle and
reshuffle them indefinitely, and to change the classification of the facts recorded on them, according to
the various tentative hypotheses with which you will
need successively to compare these facts. Another
reason against the note-book is that notes recorded
in a book must necessarily be entered in the order
in which they are obtained: and it is vitally important, in your subsequent consideration of the notes,
to be set free from the particular category in which
you have found any particular set of facts, whether
of time or place, sequence or co-existence. In sociology, as in mineralogy, "conglomerates" have always
to be broken up, and the ingredients separately dealt
with.

Upon the separate sheets should be clearly written,
so that other persons can read them, and according
to a carefully devised system (which will differ from
investigation to investigation), with as much precision as possible, and in sufficient detail, a statement
of each of the facts, or assumed facts, whether the
knowledge of them has been acquired by personal
observation, by the use of documents, by the perusal
of literature, by the formal taking of evidence, by
the interview, or by the statistical method, or in any
other way. A good deal of the ease and rapidity of

the investigation, and no small part of its fruitfulness and success, will depend on the way in which the notes are—to use a printer's word—displayed; as to which our experience suggests the following rules.

On each sheet of paper there should appear one date, and one only; one place, and one only; one source of information, and one only. Less easy of exact application, because less definite, and more dependent on the form of the provisional breaking-up and classification of the facts, is the rule that only one subject, or one category of facts, even only a single fact, should be recorded on each sheet. Of almost equal importance with this primary axiom of "one sheet, one subject-matter"—we may almost say "one sheet, one event in time and space"—is the manner in which the fact is "displayed" on the paper. Here what is of importance is identity of plan among all the hundreds, or even thousands, of sheets of notes. The date (in the study of social institutions usually the year suffices) should always appear in the same place on all the sheets—say, at the right-hand top corner of the paper; and the source of information, or authority for the statement, in the left-hand margin. The centre of the sheet will be occupied by the text of the note, that is, the main statement or description of the fact recorded, whether it be a personal observation of your own, an extract from a document, a quotation from some literary source, an answer given in evidence, a statistical calculation, a list of names or places, or a table of figures. Some of the sheets may record additional

hypotheses that have suggested themselves, for subsequent comparison with the facts; or even a "general
impression", or a summary of a group of facts,
given in addition to a note on a separate sheet of
each of the facts themselves. On what part of the
sheet to write the name of the place at which the
event occurred, and what headings and sub-head-
ings should be added by way of classification, constitutes the central puzzle-question with which the
investigator is confronted in devising, for any systematic investigation, the system for his note-taking.
This cannot be definitely determined, in any elaborate or extensive investigation, except in conjunction
with the provisional classification or the successive
classifications that may be adopted during the enquiry. Assuming that the investigation is concerned
with all the social institutions of one place, and with
no other places, the name of the place can, of course,
be taken for granted, and not recorded on the innumerable sheets (except in so far as it may be
necessary for the convenience of other persons using
the same notes, when it may be given by the use of
an india-rubber stamp once for all). In such an
investigation the principal heading, to be placed in
the centre of the top of the sheet, may be the name
or title of the particular organisation to which the
note relates, whilst the sub-heading (which can be
best put immediately under the date on the right-
hand side) may denote the particular aspect of the
organisation dealt with, whether it be, for instance,
some feature of its constitutional structure, or some

incident of its activities. If, on the other hand, the investigation is concerned with social institutions in different places, the name of the place at which each event takes place becomes an essential item of the record, and it should be placed in a prominent position, either in the centre of the page at the top, or as the first sub-heading on the right-hand side beneath the date. The one consideration to be constantly kept in view, in this preliminary task of deciding how to record the facts that constitute the subject-matter of the enquiry, is so to place the different items of the record—the what, the where, the when, and the classification or relationship—that in glancing rapidly through a number of sheets the eye catches automatically each of these aspects of the facts. Thus, a carefully planned "display", and, above all, identity of arrangement, greatly facilitates the shuffling and reshuffling of the sheets, according as it is desired to bring all the facts under review into an arrangement according to place, time, or any other grouping. It is, indeed, not too much to say that this merely mechanical perfection of note-taking may become an instrument of actual discovery.

"What is the use of this pedantic method of note-taking, involving masses of paper and a lot of hard thinking, not to mention the shuffling and re-shuffling, which is apparently the final cause of this intolerable elaboration?" will be asked by the post-graduate student eager to publish an epoch-making treatise on the *Art of Government*, or, perchance, on the *History of Liberty*, within the two years he has allotted to the taking of his doctorate. The only answer we can give is to cite our own experience.

The "Webb speciality" has been a study, at once historical and analytic, of the life-history of particular social institutions during the last three or four centuries, such as the trade union and co-operative movements in the United Kingdom, and English local government. In these successive tasks we have been confronted, not with the constitution and activities of one organisation, in one particular year, in one part of the kingdom; but with a multiplicity of organisations, belonging, it is true, to the same genus or species, but arising, flourishing, and disappearing in diverse social environments, at different intervals throughout a considerable period of time, exhibiting a great variety of constitutions and functions, subject to successive waves of thought and emotion, and developing extensive relations with other institutions or organisations within the British community, and in some cases throughout the world. The task before us was to discover, for instance, in the tangled and complicated undergrowth of English local government, the recurrent uniformities in constitution and activities showing the main lines of development, together with all the varieties of structure and function arising in particular places, in particular decades, or within peculiar social environments; some to survive and multiply, others to decay and disappear. The main sources of our information were, as it happens, records and persons located in the various towns and villages of England and Wales, sources which, for reasons of time and expense, had each to be exhausted in a single visit. But even if all this mass of manuscript and printed records, and the hundreds of separate individuals concerned, had been continuously at our disposal, whenever we cared to consult them, it would still have been desirable to adopt a method of note-taking which would allow of a mechanical breaking-up of the conglomerates of facts yielded by particular documents, interviews, and observations, in order to reassemble them in another order revealing new co-existences or sequences, and capable of literary or statistical expression. The simplest (and usually the least fertile) way of expressing the results of an investigation is to follow strictly the chronological order in which the events have occurred, not according to their connections with other events, but exclusively according to the dates of their happening. But even for this narrow purpose the conglomerate note-book is an impossible instrument, none the less so when the subject-matter happens to be the life-history of a single and unique organisation, because the dates are never all to be found in one document, and are practically never given in one and the same strictly chronological order. In our investigations, dealing as they did with the life-history of thousands of distinct organisations, the data for which were to be found in innumerable separate documents, pamphlets, newspapers, or books, or were discovered in many observations and interviews, the conglomerate note-book system would have involved disentangling and rewriting, from all the separate note-books, every note relating to a particular year, a particular organisation, or a particular place, or indicating a particular relationship. By adopting our method of one sheet for one subject, one place, and one date, all the sheets could be rapidly reshuffled in chronological order; and the whole of our material might have been surveyed and summarised exclusively from the standpoint of chronology. But as a matter of fact, we had to use the facts gathered from all these sources, not for one purpose only but for many purposes: for describing changes in the constitutional form, or the increase or variation in the activities of the organisation; or the localisation of particular constitutions or activities in particular areas, or the connection of any of these groups of facts with other groups of facts. By the method of note-taking here described, it was practicable to sort out all our thousands of separate pieces of paper according to any, and successively according to all, of these categories or combinations of categories, so that, for instance, we could see, almost at a glance, to what extent the thousands of parish vestries that served as local authorities in the eighteenth and early nineteenth centuries were entangled in the court leet structure; in what particular year they began to apply for Acts of Parliament closing or opening their constitutions; whether this constitutional development was equally characteristic of the statutory bodies of commissioners set up

during the eighteenth century and the early part of
the nineteenth century; whether, and exactly when
and why the Referendum and the Initiative were
introduced and for what purpose; or at what stage
of development and under what set of conditions all
these authorities ceased to rely for officials on the
obligatory services of citizens and began to employ
persons at wages. Or, to take an example from our
investigations into trade unionism, it was only by
interminably arranging and rearranging our separate sheets of paper that we could ascertain how far
piece-work, or the objection to piece-work, was characteristic of a particular kind of industry, or of a particular type of trade union, or of a particular district
of the United Kingdom, or of a particular stage of
development in the organisation concerned, or of the
trade union movement as a whole. Indeed, it is not
too much to say that in all our work we have found
this process of reshuffling the sheets, and reassem-
bling them on our work-table according to different
categories, or in different sequences—a process entirely dependent on the method of arrangement of
the notes—by far the most fertile stage of our investigations. Not once, but frequently, has the
general impression with regard to the co-existence or
sequence of events with which we had started our
enquiry, or which had arisen spontaneously during
the examination of documents, the taking of oral
evidence, or the observation of the working of an
organisation, been seriously modified, or completely
reversed, when we have been simultaneously con-

fronted by all the separate notes relating to the point at issue. On many occasions we have been compelled to break off the writing of a particular chapter, or even of a particular paragraph, in order to test, by reshuffling the whole of our notes dealing with a particular subject, a particular place, a particular organisation, or a particular date, the relative validity of hypotheses as to cause and effect.[1] It may be added, parenthetically, that we have found this "game with reality", this building up of one hypothesis and knocking it down in favour of others that had been revealed or verified by a new shuffle of the notes—especially when we had severally "backed" rival hypotheses—a most stimulating recreation! Not infrequently, this playing with a sheaf of notes would result in the discovery of a new and slightly different interpretation of the facts which left the *amour propre* of both parties intact! In that way alone have we been able to "put our bias out of gear", and to make our order of thought correspond,

---

[1] An instance may be given in which we found the absolute necessity of the "separate sheet" system. Among the many sources of information from which we constructed our book, *The Manor and the Borough*, were the hundreds of reports on particular boroughs made by the Municipal Corporation Commissioners in 1835. These four huge volumes are well arranged and very fully indexed; they were in our own possession; we had read them through more than once; and we had repeatedly consulted them on particular points. We had, in fact, used them as if they had been our own bound note-books, thinking that this would suffice. But, in the end, we found ourselves quite unable to digest and utilise this material until we had written out every one of the innumerable facts with regard to certain features of the organisations on a separate sheet of paper, so as to allow of the mechanical absorption of these sheets among our other notes; of their successive assortment according to various categories; and of their being shuffled and reshuffled to test hypotheses as to suggested coexistences and sequences.

not with our own prepossessions, but with the order of things discovered by our investigations.

We realise how difficult it is to convince students —especially those with a "literary" rather than a "scientific" training—that it is by just this use of such a mechanical device as the shuffling of sheets of notes, and just at this stage, that the process of investigation often becomes fertile in actual discoveries. Most students seem to assume that it is the previous stage of making observations and taking notes which is that of discovery. We can only speak from our own experience, of which two examples may be given. When we had actually completed and published our *History of Trade Unionism* (1894) after three years' collection of facts from all industries in all parts of the kingdom, which we had arranged more or less chronologically, we found to our surprise that, apart from the vague generalities in common use, we had no systematic and definite theory or vision of how trade unionism actually operated, or what exactly it effected. It was not until we had completely re-sorted all our innumerable sheets of paper according to subjects, thus bringing together all the facts relating to each subject, whatever the trade concerned, or the place, or the date—and had shuffled and reshuffled these sheets according to various tentative hypotheses—that a clear, comprehensive, and verifiable theory of the working and results of trade unionism emerged in our minds, to be embodied, after further researches by way of verification, in our *Industrial Democracy* (1897).

A further instance occurred in connection with the
work of one of us on the Poor Law Commission in
1907. It had been commonly assumed on all sides
that the Local Government Board and its predecessors had continued throughout to administer the
"principles of 1834". Upon insistence on actual examination of the policy pursued through the seventy
years that had elapsed since 1834, one of the Commissioners was deputed to report what had been
done. This involved the examination of every manifestation of policy, such as the successive statutes,
general orders, special orders, official circulars, etc.,
numbering in all some thousands, and nearly all of
them dealing not with one but with many different
points. These were all analysed by subject, date, and
place, on innumerable sheets of paper. To these data
was added a similar analysis of the letters of the
Local Government Board and its predecessors, from
1835 to 1906, addressed to a dozen of the principal
Boards of Guardians (the analysis being made by
permission of these authorities from their own letter-
books), as well as their own records of the inspector's
verbal decisions and advice on his various visits.
When this task was completed, neither the able assistants who had done the work, nor we who had
directed it, had the least idea what the policy on
each subject had been at each period. It was not
until the sheets had been sorted out, first according
to subjects, and then according to dates, that the
fact and the character of a continuous gradual evolution of policy could be detected, differing from class

to class of paupers; until, in 1907, each class had come to be dealt with according to particular principles peculiar to that class, all of which were obviously very different from those of 1834. The report of this investigation was duly presented to the Poor Law Commission, with the interesting result that we heard no more of the "principles of 1834"! It was subsequently published by us as *English Poor Law Policy* (1910) and the substance of it was included, elaborated and verified, in our *English Poor Law History: the Last Hundred Years* (1929).

APPENDIX (EXAMPLES OF NOTES)

Two Sample Notes.

NEWCASTLE.

TOWN COUNCIL.

1900
Audit.

Interview.

Rodgers,
T. Cr. &
Chairman
Bd. of Gns.

Got himself elected People's Auditor about 1887, in order to exclude a worthless man. For many years the Auditors had been re-elected without question—in 1886 a worthless man, who lived by his wits, got himself nominated at last moment, on the chance of the existing holders not taking the trouble to be formally nominated. And so got elected, for the sake of the small emolument.

Rodgers, then on the *Evening News*, got himself nominated the following year, and held it for 5 years. Found out many irregularities which he exposed in *Evening News*—principal being the failure to collect the contributions of owners towards Private Improvements (paving streets)—there was £40,000 outstanding on which owners were paying no interest, whilst Corporn was borrowing the money at interest. Corporation then turned him out of the Auditorship. He had had to fight the election every year and lost it at last.

Recently he had been elected a Councillor. Was not satisfied with the way the business was done. Would prefer L.G.B. audit.

NEWCASTLE

TOWN COUNCIL.

1892.

Committee's
Newcastle Imp. Act. 1892.

Proceedings.

Aug. 4. 1892. p. 568.

Council Resolves:

"That the powers & duties of the Council under Part 9 (Sanitary Provisions), Part 10 (Infectious Diseases), and Part 11 (Common Lodging Houses) of the N'castle-upon-T. Improvement Act 1892 be delegated to the Sanitary C'tee, until 9 Nov. next or until the Council otherwise direct."
Similarly Powers relating to Streets, Buildings, and Plans are delegated to Town Imp. C'tee.

CHAPTER V

THE investigator into social institutions, as we have noticed, is necessarily without the aid of the instruments which are at the disposal of the physicist or the chemist. Nor can he, like the biologist, put his specimens on the dissecting table. But the social investigator has some compensatory advantages. His subject-matter, unlike the subject-matter of his fellow-workers in other sciences, is an entity endowed with quite peculiar "language and writing habits"; habits yielding rich deposits of records about past and contemporary events which would be unobtainable by the methods of personal observation and statistical measurement. But not all manuscript or printed matter has evidential value: it is the mark of the ignoramus to believe a statement because he sees it in print. Moreover, in order to become what the social investigator recognises as original sources (as distinguished from writings based on sources) the written word must originate in personal observation or personal participation. "I see a time coming", said Ranke, "when we shall build modern history no longer on the accounts even of contemporary historians, except where they possessed original knowledge, much less on derivative writers, but on the relations of eye-witnesses and the original documents."[1]

THE DISTINCTION BETWEEN DOCUMENTS AND CONTEMPORARY LITERATURE

Now these manuscript and printed sources fall under two distinct heads; documents and contemporaneous literature. We quite frankly put our own separate and distinct meanings on these two terms; our excuse being that the definitions of the words "document" and "literature" to be found either in current treatises on the methodology of history, or in modern dictionaries are not helpful, and are, indeed, mutually destructive.[2] What is essential is to affix to

[1] Quoted in *The History and Historians in the Nineteenth Century*, by G. P. Gooch, 1913, p. 88.

[2] "Documents", we are told by the most widely read writers on the study of history, "are the traces which have been left by the thoughts of men of former times." (*Introduction to the Study of History*, by Charles Langlois and Charles Seignobos, translated by G. G. Berry, 1898; see also *La Methode Historique appliquée aux sciences sociales*, by Charles Seignobos, 1911); or "a document is a trace left by fact", a characteristic shared by not only all literary matter, but also by science, music, arts, roads, canals, houses, ships, and machinery. On the other hand, it is authoritatively stated in the *New Oxford Dictionary* that "a document is an instrument on which is recorded, by means of letters, figures, or marks, matter which may be evidentially used;" whilst "Literature" is "the body of writings produced in a particular country or period, or in the world in general", or "in a more restricted sense . . . writing which has claim to consideration on the ground of beauty of form or emotional effect". Thus, if we accept the wider of these two definitions of literature the documents of a period will be merely a specialised part of its literature; if, on the other hand, we choose the narrower sense some documents will be literature and others not. Neither these nor any other of the current definitions seem to us illuminating to the student of social organisation.

each of the terms selected a meaning which will make clear to the student the relative values and complementary characteristics of the two main sources of the historian. The distinction which has arisen in our minds, in the day-by-day work of research, between "documents" and "literature" is the one which distinguishes between these two sources of information *according to the origin and purpose of their creation*; origins and purposes which determine their respective values as evidence for the reconstruction and the representation of the past events. *A document, in our definition, is an instrument in language which has, as its origin and for its deliberate and express purpose, to become the basis of, or to assist, the activities of an individual, an organisation, or a community.* According to this definition all written executive orders, warrants, plea-rolls, business diaries, minutes of proceedings, accounts, customs' returns, registers, rules, statutes, byelaws, charters, constitutions, proclamations, and treaties are documents. They are not written with any view to inform historians or sociologists, or other persons unconcerned with the activities in question. They are, in fact, secreted exclusively for the purpose of action. They are, in a sense, facts in themselves, not merely the representation of facts. The word, "literature", we shall use for all other contemporaneous writings yielding information as to what purport to be facts, whether such writings originate in the desire for the intellectual, emotional, or artistic self-expression, or for the purpose of describing and communicating to others any real or imagined event. Hence, on the one hand, we exclude from the term "literature" all documents in our sense, however perfect in literary form these documents may be; and we include on the other, so far as they can be made to yield anything useful to the social student, scientific treatises, sermons, newspapers, and pamphlets, poems, plays, biographies, and autobiographies, novels and all the myriad varieties of books of every description, the great majority of which have no claim, on the ground of beauty of form or emotional effect, to be "literature" in the narrower sense. Whether beautiful or not, they are included by us as literature whenever they yield contemporaneous testimony as to the organisation or the events into which we are enquiring.[1]

For the purpose of illustrating in practical detail

[1] Something like this definition with regard to different types of sources has been suggested by Bernheim. "Sources are the results of human proceedings which are either originally intended, or which are specially suited by their existence, origin, and other relations for the purpose of making known or testifying to historical facts. . . . Among them we distinguish two groups, first, remains in the narrow sense, which, without any intention of information, are surviving parts of the proceedings and activities themselves. . . . Secondly, memorials which are specially intended for the information of interested persons, such as records, inscriptions, etc." (*Lehrbuch der historischen Methode*, by Ernst Bernheim, 1908, pp. 252-256.)

We attach no importance to my selection of the terms "documents" and "contemporaneous literature" to denote the two main sources of historical information. At one time we thought "archives" would be a better term than "documents," but seeing that the word "archive" has always been associated with documents of state (the word "archive" having at first been used for the public building or receptacle in which the documents were kept), it seemed a contradiction in terms to apply this word also to the minutes and accounts, say, of a gambling club or of a secret revolutionary sect. And yet the business records of these types of social organisation must be included from the standpoint of the sociologist in the same class of sources as the minutes and accounts of a government department, a municipality, a trade union, or a co-operative society. It would the relative yield in quality and quantity from these two distinct sources of information, we are again driven into the narrow corner of our own investigations. During the ten years spent on our researches into eighteenth century English local government, we were confronted with an inexhaustible assortment both of documents and of literature. In the way of documents there were not only the usually well-preserved, though seldom printed, voluminous records of the three hundred municipal corporations and quarter sessions of county justices, but also, scattered in churches and rectories, public buildings

help clearness of thought if a scholar with an encyclopaedic knowledge of all kinds of history would overhaul the whole terminology of historical methodology so as to get clear lines of demarcation between such terms as sources, original sources, inedited sources, texts, printed texts, documents, material documents, human documents, rolls, muniments, state papers, records, archives, inscriptions, contemporaneous literature, current histories and treatises, and other "books about books". Such an authority might perhaps explain when a modern document ceases to be "original" and becomes a "printed text"; for instance, an agenda for a Cabinet meeting printed overnight. We suggest that there is no such thing in modern society as an "original" document in the old sense, its place being taken, as Mr. Hubert Hall remarks, by "printed editions". (See *Studies in English Official Historical Documents*, by Hubert Hall, 1908, p. 50; *Historical Evidence*, by H. B. George, 1909.)

It is unnecessary to point out that there are always border-line cases, as with all definitions. For instance, whilst the ordinary legal text-book cannot be considered a document, some types of law books may have been prepared with the express purpose of determining action in particular courts. What is more important is that one written instrument may be a document for the study of the organisation from which it issues, and literature for the study of other organisations incidentally described or referred to by the author of the document. For instance, an eighteenth century archdeacon's charge is a document for the historian of the English Church of that period; it is literature with regard to facts given incidentally about the poor law activities of the parish or the customs of the manor. Or to take a more modern example, Mr. Bernard Shaw's play, *Heartbreak House*, is a document for the history of the British stage, but it is merely literature for the description of that unique social institution, the English country house.

and solicitors' offices throughout England and
Wales, the surviving manuscript minutes and accounts of more than ten thousand parish vestries;
the presentments and findings of innumerable juries
of different sorts; the rolls of countless manors and
manorial boroughs; and towards the middle of our
period, the manuscript proceedings of the rapidly
increasing class of statutory authorities for special
purposes. Added to the mass of manuscript secreted
by these tens of thousands of local authorities for the
guidance of their own activities, there was a more
limited class of documents connected with the sub-
ordination of all these authorities to the national
government, such as the voluminous general and
local Acts of Parliament, the official reports of legal
cases, the orders of the Privy Council, the corre-
spondence between the Secretary of State and the
county justices or the municipal corporations, not
to mention the proceedings of Parliament itself and
the reports of select committees and royal commissions. The sources that we include as literature were
even more unfathomable, seeing that they comprised, potentially, the whole body of eighteenth
century publications. But our successive soundings
of this illimitable ocean satisfied us that, in these
publications, the richest deposits of facts as to local
government were to be found, not in the works of
the historians, even the historians of particular
towns or countries, but (to give them in the order
of their yield) in (a) the contemporary legal text-
books (more especially in the footnotes or prefaces

giving the personal experience of the authors as justices of the peace or stewards of the manor); (*b*) in the mass of polemical pamphlets so characteristic of the century; (*c*) in provincial newspapers and in certain London periodicals; together with (*d*) manuscript or published letters, diaries, biographies, and travels. We gradually discovered that each class of local authority had its special affiliations with the surrounding mass of literature. The charges of archdeacons and bishops, and sometimes even their sermons, threw unexpected light on the civil constitution and activities of the parish, even if this was outside the jurisdiction of ecclesiastical authority; whilst the essays, plays, and novels of Addison, Steele, Gay, Fielding, Smollett, Goldsmith, Sterne, Sheridan, and less known authors were found sometimes to abound, not only in vivid caricatures of county and parish officers, but also in casual allusions and incidents which elucidated or amplified the bare facts embedded in the minutes of vestries and in the orders of quarter sessions.

THE USE OF DOCUMENTS

The conclusions reached by us as to the utilisation of documents and literature respectively are given with a certain hesitation. Each branch of sociology may have its own particular use of documents and literature. The methods of research necessary and appropriate to a study of the life-history of social institutions may be either impracticable or insufficient for accounts of the lives of great men, or for the chronicles of wars and dynasties, or for the descriptions of unique events, such as the negotiation of a treaty or the outbreak of a revolution. Whatever may be the requirements of other branches of sociology, we can say with confidence that, for our own speciality—the analytical history of the evolution of particular forms of social organisation—an actual handling of the documents themselves must form the very foundation of any reconstruction or representation of events, whether of preceding periods or of the immediate past.[1]

There is, it will be noted, no such object of study as the present, which is a mere point between two eternities. What we investigate is, when we investigate it, a series of events which have already happened, though some of them may have only very recently happened, together with the inferences that we may draw as to events which may hereafter happen. Thus it is, strictly speaking, only the past and the future with which the investigator is concerned; and

[1] The exact date, authenticity, meaning of the terms used, and even the personal authorship of a document, are matters for research by the historian whether of ancient times or of recent events. In our investigations into comparatively modern social organisation the date, authenticity, and meaning of the terms used are seldom in question, whilst the personal authorship of a document is usually unknown, and in nearly all cases irrelevant to our investigation. On the other hand, the multiplicity of modern documents makes it impossible to follow the advice (given in Mr. Hubert Hall's admirable *Studies in English Official Historical Documents*, 1908, p. 2) that "we must examine, if we do not utilise, every known historical document that concerns the period or subject under treatment, and we should, for the purpose of estimating the value of the evidence available, even take into account such documents as are known to have formerly existed". The historian of modern institutions needs usually to adopt the device of "sampling", subsequently described.

it is only the documents, the writings secreted for the purpose of action, that yield authoritative evidence of the facts about the constitution and the activities of the social institutions to be studied. Hence the first question must be: where are the documents of the organisation, and how can I get at them? If the documents are inaccessible, the subject is impracticable.[1] The order in which you examine the several documents may be dictated by the order in which you can gain access to them. But as a general rule it is well to begin with such of the documents as discover the outer framework of your subject. The most notable of these are the general statutes and the common law within which the

[1] We gladly place on record that, in our own researches, we have experienced little difficulty in getting at the documents. We can in fact recall only two refusals of access. One was that of a great landed proprietor in respect to the rolls of one of his manorial courts, a refusal afterwards explained to us by the fact that he was engaged in a lawsuit with the Crown about mineral rights and regarded us not as historians but as socialist detectives for the Treasury case! The other instance was that of a trade union official who refused us access to the records of his organisation on the ground that he himself was going to write the history of the union, a task which he never accomplished.

It is one of the difficulties in the way of investigation of profit-making enterprise that the utmost secrecy is almost always maintained with regard to its documents, particularly cost accounts, selling prices, and profit and loss accounts.

We may note that we have never paid any fee for consulting official records other than those of the Registrar-General of Births, Marriages, and Deaths; though a modest gratuity to the attendant who has had the trouble of bringing the volumes is not out of place. The Clerk of the Peace in charge of quarter sessions' records has, in the past, occasionally asked for a substantial fee, which we have always refused to pay. This practice has now, we believe, been abandoned, even by Clerks of the Peace. The incumbents of innumerable parishes have willingly produced without fee the vestry minutes or churchwardens' accounts in their custody; although we believe that they, according to custom, usually charge a fee for allowing extracts from the registers of baptisms, marriages, and burials, which we have never needed to inspect.

organisation is assumed to work. The local Acts, on the other hand, so characteristic of the British organisations of the eighteenth and early nineteenth centuries, can only be understood in close connection with the documents (and even with the literature) of the voluntary associations or the local authorities which have promoted this form of legislation. But whatever may be the character of the documents, there is one rule to which there should be no exception. Any mere summary or abstract of a document, however skilfully made, is worthless as a source. In our view the only safe place for summaries and abstracts is the waste-paper basket. What the social investigator must always insist on is the original document or an exact verbatim copy. The value of extracts from documents, as distinguished from abstracts, depends, it is obvious, on the accuracy, intelligence, and exact purpose of the extractor. When these factors are unknown, quotations from documents—for instance, those frequently given in local histories, or in contemporary pamphlets and newspapers—are worthless for the main purpose of research, that is, the discovery, *in their right proportion*, of all the facts about the constitution and activities of a particular type of organisation. But assuming accurate transcription, these stray extracts may be effectively used as additional illustrations of facts already discovered by a personal examination of the original documents of similar organisations. Whatever may be the experience of other kinds of historians, for the scientific investigator into social organisation there is no possible alternative to the examination of the documents themselves by the persons or groups of persons engaged in the enquiry.

The question now arises of how to approach and handle the very considerable mass of documents that exist relating to recent history, and, in England at any rate, especially the history of the last two or three centuries.[1] The conditions under which our own investigations have been carried on are, as already indicated: (*a*) that the documents of each separate organisation could usually not be re-examined, and they had therefore to be worked through once and for all; (*b*) that these researches into hundreds of separate organisations in different parts of the country had to be carried on, not by one person but by a small group of persons; and, (*c*) seeing that these documents were numbered by tens of thousands, that we had necessarily to proceed by the method of "sampling"—forgoing, as the biologist also must, any idea of inspection of every individual of the species concerned.

---

[1] We regret that some of the documents for eighteenth and even nineteenth century history are silently disappearing. Many of the MS. records of the eighteenth and early nineteenth centuries of vestries, manors, and statutory authorities, and even those of some of the municipal corporations, are mouldering away in the garrets of private houses and solicitors' offices or in the damp or dusty vaults of municipal authorities. The documents of trade unions are frequently destroyed when the organisation moves to a new headquarters. We have the melancholy consolation that this destruction of the documents that we have examined and used may ensure our books being continuously used for reference, not because of the value of our own work, but because they will be, in many cases, the only repository of the remnants of documents which may, in themselves, have an interest for posterity.

First and foremost among the requirements is an invariable application of the system of note-taking already described. Some provisional break-up of the subject must have been agreed on, in order that identical data for different organisations in different localities and at different dates shall appear in an identical way on the separate sheets of paper prepared at different times, or contributed to the common pool by different members of the group. But it is essential that this classification, in so far as it concerns subjects, should be provisional only; and that each investigator should be continuously on the lookout for new categories of thought, new classifications of fact, or new hypotheses as to co-existences and sequences. We quote again the paradoxical axiom: "if ye expect not the unexpected ye shall not find truth". But these notes, each of which will be confined to one fact or event at a single date, are not sufficient for the work of the investigator into documents extending continuously over a long period of years. There are some facts which have as their characteristic the element of continuous happening. For example, it is essential to know whether the governing body of an organisation changes in composition, and how it changes: what proportion of its members attend and how frequent are its meetings. Further, there are some perpetually recurring facts, which are individually unimportant, but the recurrence or non-recurrence of which over particular periods of years has an importance of its own. This fact of recurrence or non-recurrence cannot be recorded on sheets which are each limited to one date. In such cases, the fact of recurrence and the frequency of the recurrence must be recorded, for a specified period, on a separate sheet of paper. And assuming that a particular organisation has many activities, *the changing proportion from time to time between these activities is an important feature of its growth*. For all these reasons it is necessary that the investigator should keep by him in his work a series of note-sheets, on which he can, at intervals among his relentless noting of separate facts, from time to time summarise qualitatively as well as quantitatively the successive amendments of the constitution, changes in the social status and in the general outlook of representatives, officials, and members respectively; or the gradual waxing or waning of the several activities, or the successive phases of the relations of the organisation to other organisations and to the community at large. In short, though each investigator's sheaf of notes will, in the main, represent a breaking-up according to date, there must be, complementary to this statistical analysis, a dynamical analysis summarising the facts as a process in time. Finally, it is useful to encourage each investigator to note down, on completing his reading of the records of each institution for each decade or so, whilst the facts are still fresh in his memory, his unstudied, and perchance inconsistent and puzzled, impressions of the organisation, in comparison with other organisations of the same type, in different places or at other periods. What you know that you do not know about an organisation, that is to say, a new puzzle-question, becomes in itself an instrument of research.

THE METHOD OF SAMPLING DOCUMENTS

We pass now to a problem in sociological research which is peculiar to the investigation, not of one institution or association, but of a whole genus of social organisation, comprising innumerable separate social institutions susceptible of classification in species or sub-species according to their respective origins and characteristic lines of development. In our own case it was clearly impracticable, even if we had been willing to devote the time and could afford the necessary secretarial assistance, to examine the manuscript records of all the tens of thousands of local authorities that made up the multifarious and tangled undergrowth of English government in the eighteenth and early nineteenth centuries. Moreover, early in our investigations we discovered that if we made no intelligent selection of specimens, we were doing merely repetition work, the documents of one authority after another repeating, with quite amazing uniformity, all the features that we had already discovered and recorded in previous specimens.[1] But how were we to know in advance which hamlet, parish, borough, city, or county might yield in its records a new variety of

[1] "When no thought whatever occurs to you upon the facts that you are observing, it becomes useless to go on heaping up additional observations." (*Wie studirt man Sozialwissenschaft*, by Josef Schumpeter, Munich, 1915.)

manor or vestry, sessions or jury, officer or council, sewers commission or statutory body for special purposes: a variety which was not a mere freak, but a new species exemplifying one of the main lines of growth of local government? We found the solution in a process of sampling. Now there are many ways of sampling. In an investigation into the statical conditions of a particular section of the population the most accurate form of sampling is to extract, in a purely mechanical way, a series of examples from the mass; for instance, to examine in detail every twentieth street, house, family, or individual, taking them strictly as they come. But this process assumes a certain uniformity among the units within a particular area at a given time. Another way is to take samples at specific intervals during a period of time. Or the investigator may trust to all sorts and kinds of indications that new species are likely to be discovered in particular localities, at particular periods, or under particular conditions. In the case of the social institutions with which we were directly concerned the mere arithmetical sampling was too laborious, for if we had taken a sufficient proportion of the enormous number of local authorities—a number running into several tens of thousands—to make this device trustworthy, it would have transcended our powers of investigation. Hence we had usually to fall back on indirect methods of sampling according to indications afforded either by the documents of the national government or by contemporaneous literature.

We had no need of the device of sampling in the
case of the constitution and activities of "the Rulers
of the County". The Lord-Lieutenant, the sheriff,
and the justices of the peace were not only governed,
from Northumberland to Cornwall, from Kent to
Glamorgan, by one and the same system of statute
law, but they were also each and all appointed by
the Crown, and all alike carried on their daily
administration under the direction of the Assize
Judges and the Secretary of State. These central
authorities were not unduly numerous. As regards
the counties themselves, it was not beyond our
powers, in the course of several years, to go through
the manuscript records of as many as two-thirds
of all the counties of England and Wales; and we
naturally included in this large assortment counties
such as Middlesex and Lancashire, the administration of which was notoriously extensive and peculiar,
as well as the smaller or wholly rural counties. Nor
had we any great difficulty in deciding how to deal
with the three or four hundred municipal corporations and manorial boroughs. The exceptionally
massive volumes of the famous Royal Commission
of 1835, supplemented by the small but steadily
increasing crop of published archives and town
histories, gave us the necessary information for
tentatively classifying these corporations in clearly
defined species, so that we could select leading
specimens for detailed investigation of their manuscript minutes and other documents. Our principal
difficulty lay in discovering the method of sampling

the two forms of English local government, which, as it happened, were peculiarly characteristic of the period between the Revolution of 1689 and the Municipal Corporations Act of 1835, namely, government by the parish vestry and government by statutory authorities for special purposes. The variegated government of the ten or fifteen thousand parishes and townships, extending from one end of the kingdom to the other, was nominally based on the meeting of "inhabitants in vestry assembled", exercising an immemorial right to raise an unlimited rate or tax for any public purpose. But our earliest investigations revealed that the actual constitution and powers of this government in different parishes showed a baffling variety, and were derived indifferently from prescription, bishop's faculty, canon law, general statute, local Act, dictatorial assumption of the principal inhabitants, and even surreptitious inheritance from the decaying manorial court. Meanwhile the new statutory authorities for special purposes were springing up all over the country in ports and cities, in the new manufacturing districts, and even in lonely wilds of moor and mountain—for the maintenance of turnpike roads, for the management of ports and harbours, for paving, cleansing, and lighting the streets, for police, for markets, for sewers, for poor relief—each with its own distinctive constitution and peculiar functions. Sometimes these authorities appeared in the guise of a transformed vestry or the *ad hoc* committee of an ancient municipal corporation, but usually they had started up spontaneously as a brand new authority, originating in a voluntary association of "the principal inhabitants". In the great majority of cases these authorities eventually depended for this constitution and powers on a local Act. Now these local Acts of Parliament, literally thousands in number, which play the leading rôle in determining the structure and function of the English local government throughout the eighteenth and early nineteenth centuries, had never been systematically examined; they were not collected in any code or treatise, but were spread over literally hundreds of volumes; and they had not even been described other than very perfunctorily. They had, in fact, because of their very bulk and unpleasant aridity, been mainly ignored alike by historians and legal writers. They extended over the whole of the centuries with which we were concerned; and they were as verbose and repulsive in their language as they were varied in their substance. These legal enactments were, as Maitland said of law in general, "large fertile tracts of history which the historian has, as a rule, to avoid because they are too legal for him".[1]

Whether or not the Webbs were qualified to

[1] *Why the History of English Law is not Written*, by F. W. Maitland, 1888, an Inaugural Lecture delivered in the Arts School at Cambridge, 13th October. "Legal documents", explains Maitland, "documents of the most technical kind, are the best, often the only evidence that we have for social and economic history, for the history of morality, for history of practical religion. Take a broad subject—the condition of the great mass of Englishmen in the later Middle Ages, the condition of the villagers. That might be pictured for us in all truthful detail; its political, social,

undertake the task, it was clear that these local Acts had to be tackled. A preliminary survey, which was, in itself, no light task, revealed the fact that for each type of statutory authority there was, at each period, a fashion or model, alike in constitutional form and in powers, a model which changed from time to time, sometimes only slightly and slowly, as in the case of the turnpike trusts, but at other times suddenly and completely, as, for instance, in the constitution of the select vestries at the beginning of the nineteenth century. It was by a systematic analysis of all the local Acts for a single year, repeated at given intervals throughout more than a century, that we discovered, not only the material for a comprehensive vision of the evolution of political ideas as to the right constitution and powers of local authorities, but also valuable indications as to the whereabouts of typical specimens of each kind of authority, which could then be investigated in detail by analysis of their own minutes of proceedings or other documents. For the rest we had to rely on contemporaneous literature. Fortunately for us, the Englishmen of the eighteenth and nineteenth centuries were a quarrelsome lot,

economic, moral aspects might all be brought out; every tendency of progress or degradation might be traced; our supply of evidence is inexhaustible; but no one will extract its meaning who has not the patience to master an extremely formal system of pleading and procedure, who is not familiar with a whole scheme of actions with repulsive names." (*Ibid.*, p. 9.)

For more about English local Acts, the interested student may refer to *Statutory Authorities for Special Purposes*, by S. and B. Webb, 1922 ; *Municipal Origins*, by F. H. Spencer, 1911; *History of Private Bill Legislation*, by F. Clifford, 1887.

alternately denouncing the old and cursing the new. Hence there arose a mass of polemical pamphlets on the varieties of parish government and on the sins of omission and commission of the new statutory authorities. It was this use of contemporaneous literature that enabled us to select, from the absolutely unwieldy mass of documents, a sufficiently varied assortment of specimens of all kinds, in all parts of the country, from which to describe both the normal evolution and the exceptional developments of the local government of England and Wales.

The Use of Contemporaneous Literature

The historian who attempted to build up a representation of past events exclusively from documents in the sense in which we use that word, would resemble a physiologist who restricted himself to piecing together, from a heap of dry bones, the skeleton of the human body. For documents, whether they take the form of general statutes or local Acts, treaties or customs statistics, minutes of meetings or financial accounts, are economical in their record of facts; they tell the truth, they may tell nothing but the truth, but they never tell the whole truth. This restricted evidential value is inherent in the fact that documents, by definition, are not drawn up with the object of supplying a narrative or affording an explanation, but are secreted solely for the purpose of action. Thus, not only economy of time, trouble, and expense, but also economy in risk—the risk of superfluous responsibility, disagreement, and dissent—are governing motives in the drafting of documents. An important event may be authoritatively recorded, but what led up to the event, under what conditions it took place, what persons were concerned, what was the character of these persons, what was their behaviour and state of mind, are all categories of fact that may be said to be vividly absent from documents.[1] What the document records may be events, but, as it has been well said, "events are only the skeleton of history",[2] as they are of any study of social institutions. The only source from which the social investigator can get the information about the past that supplies to the skeleton a living body is what we have called contemporaneous literature.

To illustrate the way in which contemporaneous literature may be used to clothe with flesh and

[1] It is interesting to note that where we find extra-documentary material in documents, as in the case of the preambles to treaties and Acts of Parliament, these declaratory pronouncements bear little resemblance to the facts of the case. Such explanatory statements are documentary only in revealing what the initiators of the treaty or Act desired the public to believe. These false statements may be considered as a lubricant overcoming the friction which might otherwise impede the fulfilment of the objects desired.

[2] *History and Historians in the Nineteenth Century*, by G. P. Gooch, 1913, p. 74. It must be admitted that, as Mr. Gooch indicates, it is quite possible for the researcher, for lack of systematic planning of his investigation, with full and frequent use of classification and a wide range of varied hypotheses, together with scientific system of note-taking, to "fall into the ocean of documents and be drowned". This was said (by another historical student, Scherer) to have been the fate of Taine. "He collected a mass of details, many of them insignificant, while omitting matter of vital importance". (*Ibid.*, p. 246.) Nevertheless, Taine was a discoverer, even if not perfect as an investigator (and who is?).

blood the bare bones of facts extracted from documents, we may cite the story of Merceron, the demagogue of Bethnal Green who ruled the turbulent vestry for half a century, affording "a remarkable example of government by what the Americans have since termed a boss".[1] We originally discovered this local worthy in reading the manuscript vestry minutes of Bethnal Green for 1787; and we followed his seemingly disinterested career in the prosaic and scanty entries in the vestry records for three decades. We watched him securing the confidence of the little knot of regular attendants at the vestry meetings; getting himself placed year after year on all the committees; evidently performing much laborious work for the parish, and incidentally undertaking the onerous responsibility of keeping its funds, and all without salary or other obvious remuneration. Meanwhile we had traced him in the Crown Office archives as recommended to the Lord Chancellor for inclusion in the commission of the peace for Middlesex. From thence we followed him in the manuscript minutes of the Middlesex Quarter Sessions, again seeing him appointed on every committee for letting contracts and auditing accounts, always working in close conjunction with the more notorious Mainwaring, long Member of Parliament for the county and chairman of the quarter sessions, who presently advised the Crown to appoint Merceron as deputy chairman.

[1] For this episode, see *The Parish and the County*, pp. 79-90; and for Merceron's association with Mainwaring, see pp. 556-80.

For thirty years, whilst Merceron was making his way, there is, in the documents, no sign that anything is wrong. (We may say that we learnt from contemporary pamphlets that Merceron was actually prosecuted for peculation as early as 1813; and, though he escaped conviction, this was alleged to have been by his bribing the prosecutor's attorney to withdraw the case.) Suddenly, in 1818, the manuscript minutes of Bethnal Green record the fact that Merceron and his friends had been defeated in the election to the new vestry; and there are a series of laconic resolutions directing a criminal prosecution, which was followed by further litigation and heated local controversies extending over half a dozen years.[1]

Unfortunately, a gap in the records—those for five years being wholly missing—prevents an exact following of the events from this official source.

[1] Under the pressure of these exciting events even the manuscript minutes break into literary description, having no greater evidential value than a newspaper report. We give the following unique extract in contrast with the rule of habitual reticence:

"The greatest tumult and disorder now began to be manifest in opposition to Dr. Gwynne (who had been elected chairman), the uproar and confusion continued without intermission for more than an hour, when a scene of riot prevailed which became seriously alarming, the obvious intention of several parties present being to compel Dr. Gwynne, by main violence, to quit the chair, many persons getting upon the tables, even over the backs of others, and thus endeavouring to force their way to the top of the room to place Mr. Rennoldson in the chair. The great pressure and suffocating heat added to the vociferation and menacing attitude of various parties, caused the greatest terror and alarm in the vestry room. A cry of murder was heard, and lives of several vestrymen appearing to be in serious danger, the chairman was requested to disperse the meeting. He thereupon read the Riot Act . . . and . . . ordered the meeting in a legal way to separate . . . whereupon the officers . . . from the Police Department in Worship Street were called in. . . . The meeting was with some difficulty dispersed." (MS. Minutes, Bethnal Green, 6th February 1823.)

When the extant records begin again in 1828 we find Merceron once more in indisputable supremacy. He and his son-in-law are leading members of the select vestry: he is treasurer both of the "Watch Board" and the "Pavement Trust", he and his friends are the Commissioners of the Court of Requests; though apparently not reinstated in the commission of the peace, he is still by royal appointment a commissioner for the Land Tax and a commissioner of sewers, not only for the Tower Hamlets, but also for Westminster and for Holborn and Finsbury; he still owns and controls one-fourth of all the Bethnal Green public-houses; and his son-in-law continues salaried vestry clerk and principal executive officer of the parish. What is even more significant of his position, we find him acting always as the formal spokesman of the vestry, annually begging permission on the election day "to offer his sincere congratulations to the whole parish for the order, regularity, good feeling, and satisfaction which had been manifested by every one this day, as indeed had also been manifested by the inhabitants for the last six years, in exercising their annual elective franchise under the present Act of Parliament, for members of the select vestry, whose aim was to watch over the interest of 50,000 individuals by observing the most rigid system of economy and care in the management of our parochial affairs".

Now it so happens that the official documents for the reconstruction of the story of Merceron and Mainwaring are exceptionally full and varied, and that we were able exhaustively to examine them. But it would have been impossible to comprehend the amazing combination of brutal demagogy and ingenious peculation of the boss of Bethnal Green, and the more astute and wholesale frauds of the chairman and deputy chairman of the Middlesex bench, if contemporaneous literature had not been searched for elucidation of the laconic official records. Our richest find was a verbatim report of *The Trials at Large of Joseph Merceron, Esquire*, with appropriate prefaces describing the events leading up to his prosecution, conviction, and imprisonment, which was published with controversial objects.[1] The information given in the book related only to Merceron's criminal activities, and was mainly confined to his doings as a vestryman at Bethnal Green. For his share in the breakdown of the Middlesex bench, and also for a general account of his life and character, we had recourse to files of the contemporary London newspapers, and to an array of ephemeral pamphlets, mostly by clerical justices and incumbents of London parishes; whilst the *History of London*, by William Maitland, 1756; *The Environs of London*, by Dr. D. Lysons, 1792–1811; and a letter from Place to Hobhouse (2nd April 1928,

[1] These verbatim reports are bound up in a volume of other celebrated cases "taken in shorthand by Mr. W. S. Gurney", which were apparently a series of ventures by a publisher. These writings are an interesting example of the border line between documents and contemporaneous literature, not being official documents and having extraneous matter interposed in what purports to be a correct report of the trial, but which has no more authority than a newspaper report. Failing an official report of the proceedings, the only "document" would have been the judge's notes upon which the jury was charged.

Add. MSS. 35148, vol. i. p. 55) afforded us some
links essential to the fullness and consistency of our
narrative.

And if we pass from the demagogic and corrupt
boss of the vestry in Bethnal Green to his more
reputable contemporary, Thomas Rhodes of St.
Pancras (the great-uncle of Cecil Rhodes of South
African fame), who, after thirty years of Machia-
vellian intrigue in and outside Parliament, succeeded in extinguishing the open vestry, and in
replacing it by a close vestry made up of his
nominees, we shall see that the reconstruction of
this very typical case involved alike combination of
documents and contemporaneous literature.[1]

The documentary foundations for the narrative
were the manuscript minutes of the original open
vestry of St. Pancras, together with those of the
various statutory bodies for special purposes which
Rhodes got established by local Acts, these documents
being supplemented by the reports of select committees of the House of Commons. But all this yielded
us only the skeleton of the story. For the rise of the
little rural village into a densely crowded urban area;
for the heated discussions and disorderly episodes of
the unwieldy meetings of the inhabitants in vestry
assembled; for the coming together of the principal
inhabitants, and their support, in opposition to "the
mob", of Rhodes' machinations in the lobbies of the

[1] See *The Parish and the County.* pp. 207-11. It is interesting to note
the reflection of Rhodes' machinations in the records of other vestries,
such as Newington, Mitcham, Mile End Old Town, St. Saviour's, South-
wark.

House of Commons and in the new statutory authorities, we had to rely on contemporaneous pamphlets
and manifestos—not merely solemn statements
made by the vicar and churchwardens, or by the
leading magistrate of the neighbourhood, but also
scurrilous publications, pamphlets entitled "St.
Molly's in a Hurry, or Scribo Scratchum's Picture
of a Select Vestry" and such like, as well as on local
broadsheets and the files of London newspapers.

To fill up the gaps left by documents in what may
be termed the biographical aspect of history—the
antecedents, the contemporary circumstances, the
family connections, the character and the motives
of the leading actors—is not the sole nor even the
main usefulness of the investigator's search into contemporaneous literature. Without wide-flung netting
of this practically unbounded ocean of knowledge,
it would be impracticable to construct an imaginative presentment of the social environment in which
the various local governing authorities were embedded. We shall realise this by considering a few
cases. Nowhere in the documents of the statutory
commissions for lighting, watching, paving, and
cleansing, nor in the clauses of the local Acts to
which they owed their existence and authority,
would be found any adequate description of the
terrible conditions of disorder, dirt, and disease characteristic of the rapidly increasing urban popula-
tions of England in the latter part of the eighteenth
century. Nor would the records of the incorporated
guardians of the poor reveal the infamous state of

the workhouse or the horrors of the overseers' traffic in pauper apprentices with the capitalists of the new industries. It is not in the Crown Office archives and Home Office papers, nor in the orders of quarter sessions, that we discover the social conditions and moral standards that made possible the nefarious doings of the Trading Justices and the Bow Street runners. Equally obscure would all the official documents leave the one-idea'd philanthropy of John Howard for the prisoners,[1] or the utilitarian enthusiasm of Telford and Macadam for the reconstruction of the roads.[2] For all the atmosphere of these activities we have to trust to the testimony incidentally afforded by the swarm of contemporary journalists, pamphleteers, dramatists, novelists, verse-makers, Anglican incumbents, and Wesleyan revivalists, in which we may be steadied by the cynical judgments of the moralists and essayists, and by the matter-of-fact explanations occasionally offered by defenders of the local and central government of the time. But this is not all. Without an adequate knowledge of the writings of the eighteenth and nineteenth century political economists; without a due realisation of the great effect on the minds of a small minority of influential men produced by Jeremy Bentham and his early disciples; without a just appreciation of the peculiar combination of fervent piety and commercial individualism of Wilberforce and the "Clapham Sect", the contem-

---

[1] See *English Prisons under Local Government*, 1922, pp. 32-7.
[2] See *The Story of the King's Highway*, 1913, pp. 135-257.

porary administration of the police and prisons, of poor relief, of liquor licensing, of the suppression of nuisances, or of the incipient municipal services for the supply of water and gas, would seem no more than a whirlpool of confusion. Finally, it is through the contemporaneous literature, and not in the documents, that we are able to recognise, and then to trace, the pecuniary interests, the intellectual assumptions, and the idealistic purpose which united, as we can now see, to effect the long-drawn out transfer of the local government of England from the dying hands of a degenerate vocational organisation to those of democracies of consumers, culminating in the Municipal Corporations Act of 1835.

And here we must end this dry dissertation on the right use of historical sources, conscious that we have failed to express the joy of life to be found in these diggings into documents and soundings and nettings of contemporaneous literature. The deeper and broader the search into the sources of history, the wider the sweep from one field of discovery to another, the more fascinating becomes the craft of the social investigator. It may be doubted whether there is any sport, any game, so alluring and so continuously absorbing as the hazards of sociological research. For this craft combines a gamble for some new discovery illuminating the origin, growth, and destiny of man, with the certainty of a modest yield of facts, facts which may seem insignificant, but which may prove to be the groundwork for a stride onward into the hitherto unknown. To spend hour after hour in the chancel of an old parish church, in the veiled light of an ancient muniment room, in the hard little office of a solicitor, in the ugly and bare anteroom of the council chamber of a local authority, or even in a dungeon without ventilation or daylight (which was once our lot) with a stack of manuscripts, or a pile of printed volumes, to get through in a given time, induces an indescribably stimulated state of mind. The illusion arises that one has not one brain but several, each enjoying a life of its own. There is, first, the curiously concentrated satisfaction of the rapid rush through manuscript and printed pages, brain and hand combining to detect, and to record, from among the "common form" with which the records are filled, new features in the constitution or activities of the organisation, or unexpected reactions between it and its environment. This interest in social structure is enlivened by an exciting chase after the human factor; the discovery of the leader or leaders; the play of the hand of this man or that; the emergence in the dry annals of pecuniary self-interest, personal ambition or personal vanity; as well as of some continuously pressed policy or ideal. Meanwhile another active part of the brain is alert for indications of additional sources of information. Is there a collection of pamphlets? Is there a local news-sheet of old date, and where are the files to be found? What are the relevant biographies, autobiographies, travels, diaries, legal text-books, or other technical treatises? Once immersed in the contemporaneous literature,

a different set of faculties are called out. The temptation is no longer to skip what seems "common
form", but which might prove significant; it is rather
to wander down varied and seductive bypaths,
observing and recording what is irrelevant. From
being a detective following a dim trail, one becomes
a judge or a sorting officer, casting out false evidence
or bad material. Has the author personal knowledge, or is he merely repeating gossip or hearsay?
What exactly is his personal equation? Is one justified in using this purple patch as a description of
what actually happened, or at any rate as an illustration of the emotions roused by the happenings?
And where exactly must one stop this pleasant
browsing over newspapers and pamphlets, diaries
and law books, sermons and plays? Is it yielding
nothing but repetition and is the collection of extracts already as great as can be utilised? Meanwhile, beneath all this intense but largely automatic
activity of the intellectual craftsman, there runs the
more tranquil and deeper currents of philosophic
brooding: the underlying but continuously running
controversy between the ego that affirms and the
ego that denies. Apart from the satisfaction of
scientific curiosity, has the product social value?
Will the discovery of the past help the conduct of
the present? Assuming that we have discovered and
identified the poison secreted by the decaying vocational organisations of the eighteenth century, will
this knowledge enable the modern man to find an
antidote for similar poisons at work to-day in the

life of a trade union or a professional association? What exactly did the nation lose or gain when its local government ceased to be carried out by the unpaid personal service of its citizens as occasional overseers, haywards, and constables, and became an organisation of citizen-consumers employing at wages professional engineers, policemen, and scavengers? Would it have been possible to have retained the element of personal obligation and personal responsibility, inherent in the mediaeval corporations of agriculturists and craftsmen, within the framework of citizens' control demanded in the name of personal and political freedom? And underlying all these detailed questions there is the fundamental issue: can these secular movements of successive social expediencies be translated into ever-rising ethical values? Is morality, as it has been suggested, actually part of the nature of things?

CHAPTER VI

THE SPOKEN WORD

FOR much of his information about the social institution he is studying the investigator must rely on the oral testimony of those who know the facts. Sometimes this is available in a printed form, for instance in the voluminous questions and answers that make up nearly all the "evidence" taken by royal commissions and parliamentary committees, and published in the blue-books. Unfortunately the enormous accumulation thus enshrined—which has necessarily to be consulted—is of very varying evidential value, a shortcoming discussed in a subsequent chapter. For the greater part of his information the investigator must find his own witnesses, induce them to talk, and embody the gist of this oral testimony on his sheets of notes. This is the Method of the Interview, or "conversation with a purpose", a unique instrument of the social investigator.[1]

---

[1] The greater part of this chapter will be found, in substance, as an Appendix to *My Apprenticeship*, by Beatrice Webb, 1926, pp. 340-355. In a recently published American work, entitled *How to Interview*, by W. V. Bingham and B. V. Moore, 1931, over 300 pages are devoted to an

First, let us point out, for the benefit of students who dislike personal contacts, or who feel themselves unsuited for the difficult art of interviewing presently to be described, that this method of investigation is not required, and may, indeed, be impracticable, for historical research. It is, moreover, not absolutely essential even in the investigation of certain contemporary social institutions. Thus, English local government, from the seventeenth to the nineteenth century, was the pastime as well as the public work of potential "writing men"; of accomplished country gentlemen and ecclesiastics; of city merchants and provincial manufacturers; whilst many solicitors and barristers, and in later years medical practitioners, engineers, architects and surveyors, accountants and auditors have found in the complicated network of courts and councils a considerable part of their livelihood. Hence, as we have already shown, not only are the documents of local authorities bewildering in their number and variety, but there are also, for each generation during the past two centuries, rich deposits of fact in contemporaneous literature, in law books and treatises, in parliamentary reports and controversial pamphlets, in letters and articles in local newspapers, not to mention biographies, plays, novels, poems, and even sermons. Even the working-

elaborate description of the "personal interview" as a means of "fact-finding, informing, and motivating", largely for the instruction of Charity Organisation and other social workers, but also of teachers, salesmen or canvassers for orders, policemen, journalists, doctors, and lawyers. The book contains an extensive annotated bibliography.

class co-operative movement has, for nearly a century, had its technical periodicals, its conference and congress reports and papers, its audited accounts of trading and manufacturing enterprises, together with an incessant stream of pamphlet literature, frequently written by able intellectuals bent on informing the members and on making known to the public the achievements of the movement. On the other hand, any adequate investigation into the policy of the trade union movement during the nineteenth century, or even of the movement of to-day, would be impossible without considerable personal intercourse with the leading personalities, and even with the members of the rank and file. For the trade unions, partly because of their exclusively working-class membership, and partly because they were regarded by the law and by public opinion, even down to the last quarter of the nineteenth century, as unlawful if not actually criminal combinations, had, at the time of our investigation, neither the opportunity nor the desire to put themselves on record in contemporaneous literature, or even in office documents, more than was absolutely necessary for their immediate purposes. Moreover, the average manual worker has no love for archives. What is of "no more use" is only waste paper cumbering the narrow room. How exasperating it was to the investigator, on entering the office of a powerful modern union, or the parlour of the secretary of an ancient craft organisation, to be casually informed that "only a few months ago",

on removal to new premises, or on the occasion of
some scare about the illegality of a particular act or
decision, all the past manuscript minutes had been
destroyed, whilst the various editions of the rule-
books that had become obsolete had been burnt.
We were sometimes able to find nothing beyond
copies of the membership card and the current
rules, with possibly a few statistics of membership
for particular years. This was not always the case.
We spent many months in minutely going through
the well-kept records of (to name only some examples) the ironfounders, the boilermakers, the
stonemasons, and the London and provincial compositors. We found much of historical value in the
scantier documents of ancient trade clubs. But
though we hunted up every bit of literature or document in local libraries, trade union offices, and
members' homes—and the smallest scraps were
sometimes of fundamental importance by way of
verification—we had, for much of the past record of
the majority of the smaller unions, as well as for
their current activities, to fall back on the spoken
word. Especially for the working constitution and
day-by-day activities of the trade union movement,
had we to rely, in the main, on our innumerable
interviews with trade union officials and members,
with friendly employers and their foremen, and
with the agents of employers' associations—all this
being valuably supplemented by what we picked
up by attendance at branch or delegate meetings,
open or private, or overheard in informal inter-

course in hotel smoking-rooms, the bars of public-houses frequented by the workmen, and the homes of brain workers and manual workers in every trade, from one end of the United Kingdom to the other. The special obstacle to be overcome in this use of the interview was, in the case of the trade union movement, the presence, in all the witnesses, of unconscious bias in an aggravated form. For the ground we were exploring was, in fact, a permanent battlefield, upon which there was being waged, day in and day out, the endless secular conflict between the capitalist profit-makers and the manual working wage-earners, whilst within the ranks of each of the opposing forces there went on a continuous petty skirmishing between rival profit-makers for markets and men, and between rival unions for work and members. For this reason the process of "over-hearing" the actual transactions on each side was more valuable than any direct hearing of testimony. What we picked up in this way could be elucidated by specific enquiries, and checked for bias by investigation in other quarters, whilst we often found it possible to obtain verification of what we had learnt from scraps of documents and incidental references in contemporaneous literature that would otherwise have been without significance for us.[1]

---

[1] This paucity of documents and contemporaneous literature as sources of information for the investigator is no longer characteristic of the British trade union movement. The documents at nearly all trade union offices are nowadays voluminous and well preserved, and some of the larger unions have even regular Statistical and Research Departments. Though there is still no trade union journal analogous to *The Co-operative News*, there has been, during the past quarter of a century or so, a steadily

There are many uses of the interview. It may be a necessary passport to the inspection of documents or to an opportunity of watching, from the inside, the constitution and activities of some piece of social organisation. For this purpose the requisites are a good "introduction", brevity of statement, a modest and agreeable manner, and a ready acquiescence in any arrangement made, however inadequate or inconvenient. Above all, the student must have a clear conception of exactly which documents and what opportunities he is seeking. Do not ask for too much at the first start off; you can always ask for more; and an inch given is better than an ell refused!

But by the method of the interview is meant something more than a social gateway. The "conversation with a purpose" may be, so the American social workers say, "fact-finding", or "informing", or "motivating", according as it is designed to obtain information, to instruct or to influence the will. We use the term here solely to label a particular instrument of sociological investigation, the eliciting of facts from a competent informant by skilled interrogation. As a device for scientific investigation it is peculiar to the sociologist. It is his compensation for inability to use the astronomer's telescope or the bacteriologist's microscope.

increasing stream of monthly and quarterly periodicals published by the different unions in which the current statistics and some of the details of their work are recorded, whilst books and pamphlets on trade unionism abound. The statistical and other information compiled and published by the Government, which was, half a century ago, of the scantiest, has, since the formation of the Labour Department at the Board of Trade (now absorbed in the Ministry of Labour) been of the highest quality.

The first condition of the successful use of the interview as an instrument of research is preparedness of the mind of the operator. The interviewer should be himself acquainted not, of course, with all the known facts—that would be to set too high a standard—but with all the data that can be obtained from the ordinary text-books and blue-books relating to the subject. For instance, to cross-examine a factory inspector without understanding the distinction between a factory and a workshop, or the meaning of the "particulars clause"; or a town clerk, without knowing the difference between getting a provisional order, promoting a local Act, or working under a general Act, is an impertinence. Especially important is a familiarity with technical terms and a correct use of them. To start interviewing any specialist without this equipment will not only be waste of time, but may lead to a more or less courteous dismissal, after a few general remarks and some trite opinions; at best, the conversation will be turned away from the subject into the trivialities of social intercourse. For technical terms and technical details, relating to past as well as to present occurrences and controversies, are so many levers to lift into consciousness and expression the more abstruse and out-of-the-way facts or series of facts; and it is exactly these more hidden events that are needed to complete descriptive analysis and to verify hypotheses. And note in passing that not to have read and mastered what your client has himself published on the question is not easily forgiven!

The second condition is, of course, that the person interviewed should be in possession of experience or knowledge unknown to you. This is not to say that persons without acknowledged reputations for specialised knowledge must always be ignored; and that there should be no speculative investment in queer or humble folk. It is, for example, almost axiomatic with the experienced investigator that the mind of the subordinate in any organisation will yield richer veins of fact than the mind of the principal. This is not merely because the subordinate is usually less on his guard, and less severely conventional in his outlook. The essential superiority lies in the circumstance that the working foreman, managing clerk, or minor official is himself in continuous and intimate contact with the day-by-day activities of the organisation; he is more aware than his employer is of the heterogeneity and changing character of the facts; and he is less likely to serve up dead generalisation, in which all the living detail becomes a blurred mass, or is stereotyped into rigidly confined and perhaps obsolete categories.[1]

More difficult to convey to the student is the right manner of behaviour in interviewing.

Regarded as a method of investigation, the process of interviewing is a particular form of psycho-

[1] It is interesting to see a similar comment made about the German capitalist employer. "Hardly ever", says Professor Schumpeter, "can a business man analyse his business processes. He acts on his experience, on his feelings, and rightly so. If then we ask him about his business affairs, we get in reply any casual thought which happens to be in his mind, and to which he momentarily attaches importance." (*Wie studirt man Sozialwissenschaft*, by Josef Schumpeter, Munich, 1915, p. 427.)

analysis. From within the consciousness or sub-consciousness of another mind, the practitioner has to ferret out memories of past experience—"orders of thought" corresponding with "orders of things". You may easily inhibit free communication, or prevent the rise to consciousness of significant facts, by arousing suspicion. For instance, whilst a careful plan of examination should be prepared, no paper of questions should be apparent; and during the interview no attempt should be made to take notes. Except in cases in which your client is not merely according an interview but is consciously co-operating in your investigation, it is a mistake to bring with you a secretary or other colleague; caution is increased when a man perceives that his words are being "witnessed".

It is disastrous to "show off", or to argue; the client must be permitted to pour out his fictitious tales, to develop the most preposterous theories, or to use the silliest arguments, without demur or expression of dissent or ridicule. The competent social investigator will not look bored or indifferent when irrelevant information or trivial details are offered to him, any more than a competent medical practitioner will appear wearied by his patient's catalogue of imaginary symptoms. Accept whatever is offered: a personally conducted visit to this or that works or institution may be a dismal prospect; it may even seem waste effort to inspect machinery or plant which cannot be understood, or which has been seen *ad nauseam* before, or which is wholly irrelevant to the subject-matter of the enquiry. But it is a mistake to decline. In the course of these tiring walks and weary waitings, experiences may be recalled or elicited which would not have cropped up in the formal interview in the office. Indeed, the less formal the conditions of the interview the better. The atmosphere of the dinner-table or the smoking-room is a better "conductor" than that of the office during business hours. The best of these occasions is when you can casually start several experts arguing among themselves: in this way you will pick up more information in one hour than you will acquire during a whole day in a series of interviews.

When you have got upon confidential terms, your new friend may cite private statistics or mention unpublished documents; this should be met by an off-hand plea for permission to see them. If a direct offer be made to produce and explain documents, the interviewer has scored a notable success, and should follow it up on the spot. "I am dreadfully careless and inaccurate at figures: I wonder whether I and my secretary might come here to-morrow to look through these reports again?" will often find good-natured acquiescence.

Bear in mind that it is desirable to make the interview pleasing to the persons interviewed. It should seem to him or her an agreeable form of social intercourse. One of the authors remembers, in an early adventure in "wholesale interviewing" with a group of representative men, even telling fortunes from their hands, with all sorts of interesting results! Without such an atmosphere of relaxation, of amused interest on both sides, it will often be impracticable to get at those intimate details of daily experience which are the most valuable data of the sociologist. Hence a spirit of adventure, a delight in watching human beings as human beings quite apart from what you can get out of their minds, an enjoyment of the play of your own personality with that of another, are gifts of rare value in the art of interviewing; and gifts which are, perhaps, more frequently characteristic of the woman than of the man.

It need hardly be added that once the interview is over, the first opportunity should be taken to write out fully every separate fact or hypothesis elicited. Never trust your memory a moment longer than is necessary is an all-important maxim. Practice will make it easy to reproduce on paper, that very evening, or on the following morning before starting out for the day's work, every phrase or suggestion that needs to be recorded, even of several successive interviews.

The investigator using the method of the interview must, we need hardly say, remember his responsibilities. In any publication he must scrupulously respect the confidence accorded to him. He must invariably suppress the name of the person who has given the information. But he must do more than this. He must exercise the utmost care to prevent his identification by those familiar with him, his circumstances, his town, or his trade. Thus, it is dangerous to mention the town in which he lives; or to use such superlatives as "the oldest establishment", or "the largest factory"; or to describe any marked peculiarity of its location or layout. And there is one supreme rule which must always be observed. You must be careful never to use or publish anything to the disadvantage of your informant that he may have rashly or unsuspectingly let out in his conversation. Only by the strictest observance of these rules of discretion is the investigator's inquisition justified.

CHAPTER VII

ROYAL COMMISSIONS AND COMMITTEES OF ENQUIRY AS SOURCES FOR THE INVESTIGATOR

AT first sight it appears as if the long series of reports and proceedings of royal commissions and parliamentary or departmental committees, extending over a whole century, would afford to the social student a perfect mine of facts, about every conceivable subject of social investigation, almost dispensing with any other sources of information. Unfortunately this is not the case. It has been our lot to take part, officially or unofficially, in many enquiries of this sort; and we have analysed, or had analysed for us, the evidence given before nearly all the British commissions or committees of enquiry relating to our range of subjects. Of all recognised sources of information the oral "evidence" given in the course of these enquiries has proved to be the least profitable. Considering the time spent in listening to it, or even in rapidly reading and analysing these interminable question and answers—still more, the money spent over them—the yield of solid fact is absurdly small. This depressing conclusion was first brought home to us during our six years' investigation (1891–7) into the history, structure, and functions of British trade unionism. It happened that, in these particular years, a powerful royal commission was at work on the same subject;[1] and we awaited with impatience the publication of the evidence as a valuable means of supplementing or testing our own enquiries. It is not an exaggeration to say that the output of new fact was, so far as we personally were concerned, infinitesimal. It is, perhaps, fair to infer that the commissioners took the view that it was not their business to get at the facts. Rightly or wrongly, the commission decided, except in particular branches, to conduct its investigations by the method of oral evidence. This evidence, embodied in 96,333 questions and answers, and forming the great bulk of the published proceedings, consisted, for the most part, not of statements of fact, but of the answers to abstract conundrums put in cross-examination by the commissioners about every conceivable social or legislative reform. The greatest

---

[1] Royal Commission on Labour, first to fifth Reports, with evidence, 1892–4; *Minority Report of the Royal Commission on Labour, 1891–9, containing important proposals, etc.* (Manchester, 1894); "The Failure of the Labour Commission", by Beatrice Potter, in *Nineteenth Century*, May 1894.

"I do not think", said Lord Beaconsfield in an expansive moment, "there is anyone who more values the labour of parliamentary committees than myself. They obtain for the country an extraordinary mass of valuable information which probably would not otherwise be at hand or available; and formed, as they necessarily are, of chosen men from the two most important bodies of the state, their reports are pregnant with prudent and sagacious suggestions for the improvement of the administration of affairs." (Hansard, vol. 235, p. 1478.)

But Lord Beaconsfield was not an investigator.

triumph was, by skilful questions, to lead the witnesses, especially the working-men witnesses, into
some logical inconsistency. One or other of us attended some meetings of the commission; and it was
certainly entertaining to watch the dialecticians
"purring" at each other complacently when their
little pounces came off! But this cat-and-mouse
dialectic is not the way to discover new facts. Hence
it is hardly surprising that the royal commission,
regarded as an instrument of investigation, drew a
blank. Though the prevalence, constitution, and
working of combinations of employers and employed was one of the subjects specifically named
in the reference, the evidence taken by the commission revealed absolutely no particulars about the
number, membership, and activities of employers'
associations; whilst with regard to trade unions there
were two widely conflicting statements by witnesses
(both actually quoted in the first report), one putting the total membership at 671,000 and the other
at $1\frac{1}{2}$ millions. It was surely not beyond the com-
petence of twenty-seven commissioners, including
many distinguished intellectuals, spending three
years and £50,000 of public money, to have discovered whether the British trade union world included only 10 per cent of the workmen, or twice
that proportion. The relative advantages of piece-
work and time-work engaged a great deal of the
attention of the commissioners. But here, again, the
commissioners never even mastered the elementary
facts of the question. The student is unable to ascer-

tain whether piece-work rates or time wages were, in these years, preferred by a majority of trade unions. He cannot discover the reason why the cotton-spinners and the cotton-weavers, the coal-miners and the steel-smelters, the boot and shoe operatives and the carpet-weavers, the basket-workers and the lace-makers, were contemporaneously insisting on piece-work, and striking against attempts to substitute time wages; whereas the engineers and the cabinetmakers, the stonemasons and the ship-wrights, the ironfounders and the carpenters, regarded piece-work as the bane of their industries; and whilst other trades, again, such as the compositors and the boilermakers, appeared to be equally content with either method of remuneration. One would have thought that it would have occurred to any intelligent investigator to give up eliciting general praises of piece-work from employers, and general objections to it from operatives, in order to ascertain exactly the conditions in each case under which a particular trade union regarded piece-work as either advantageous or detrimental to the workers' interests. In fact, the hundreds of pages filled with questions and answers on the methods of remuneration, whilst affording no new light on the question, contain less accurate and less complete information than the current three-and-sixpenny manual available to the most casual student of the Labour Question. From certain vague passages in the report we gather that a majority of the commissioners had satisfied themselves of the efficacy of profit-sharing in harmonising the interest of the workmen with that of the capitalists. But nothing appears in the volumes of evidence that could, by the utmost courtesy, be called an investigation into this particular form of the wage-contract. It is true that the representatives of the co-operative movement, and one or two private profit-sharing employers, were permitted to expatiate on the advantages of their respective panaceas. An *ex parte* memorandum on the subject by Mr. (afterwards Sir) George Livesey, a member of the commission, is appended to the report. But no oral evidence as to the facts was sought for. No statistics were obtained as to the results of profit-sharing upon the total remuneration of the workers, and no information as to its effect upon trade union organisation, in the large number of firms, probably a hundred, at that time practising this method of remuneration. What is still more remarkable is that no one would gather from the proceedings of the commission that, in innumerable other instances, profit-sharing had been, for one or other unascertained reasons, after a longer or shorter trial, deliberately given up.

Or let us take the Eight Hours Day, in the early nineties the most controversial of all labour questions, and the subject to which the commission devoted most time and attention. Here, at any rate, a thorough investigation into the facts might have been expected. What everyone wanted to know was, What had been the economic results in the large number of cases in which an eight hours day had been tried? What effect did it actually have upon output and cost of production? Did wages rise or fall? Was there any increase in the number of persons employed, or was it accompanied by the introduction of additional labour-saving machinery? As the demand was for a legally prescribed eight hours day, it seemed important to discover to what extent legislative regulation of the hours of labour had been set at naught, in certain industries, by such practices as "cribbing time", and the resort to unregulated home-work. Was it true, as some declared, that legislative stereotyping of the labour day had, in some cases, positively prevented a further reduction? Further, it might have been ascertained in what way the legislative regulation of hours under the existing Factory Acts had stimulated or depressed the growth of trade unionism. An accurate statement on these points would have been of the utmost value. But on all these concrete matters there is, in the 96,333 answers, no information: a fact which may explain the anomaly that when the secretaries came to index the whole of the evidence on the Eight Hours Day they found no need for any heading as to the results of eight-hour experiments, but had to make endless entries about the "effect of (the eight hours day) *presumed or expected*".

The worthlessness of the oral evidence which made up the bulk of the commission's output was brought into strong relief by the usefulness of some of the written reports published in its proceedings.

When it came to deal with the position of the agricultural labourer, the commission delegated its investigations to a carefully selected staff of assistant commissioners, working under the direction of a skilled expert. Seventy-six typical poor law unions in England, Wales, and Ireland, and fourteen selected districts in Scotland, were chosen by the senior assistant commissioner, Mr. W. C. Little, and allotted among his twelve colleagues in such a way as to secure the most accurate diagnosis in each case. The assistant commissioners received a definite and narrowly circumscribed reference, prepared with full knowledge of what were the exact points on which information was required. From the lucid "summary report", which each was directed to prefix to his statement of facts, we watch the investigator at work. He journeys from parish to parish; holds meetings of the labourers to elicit complaints; visits the workers' cottages; hobnobs with shepherds, carters, and ploughmen in country lanes, rural markets, and auction marts; consults trade union and friendly society officials in informal chats; interviews ministers of religion of all denominations, poor law guardians and relieving officers, masters of workhouses, and inspectors of nuisances; takes counsel in the little towns with solicitors, auctioneers, estate agents, and everyone able to assist his enquiries; extracts, from the accounts of farmers, bailiffs, and landowners, actual statistics with regard to wages, perquisites, the supply of labour, the use of machinery, the prevalence of allotments, and the

labour-bill per acre for large farms and small hold-
ings respectively. The reports, as might have been
expected, vary in quality. Moreover, some bias
could not be avoided; we all have our own views,
and cannot pretend to leave them at home on our
investigation tours. But bias can be discounted. In
fact, the predominant complacency with existing
conditions that characterises these reports makes
their careful photograph of the agricultural labourer's
life revoltingly impressive. In these excellently
ordered statements the student was given, for the
first time, a definite, authoritative, and trustworthy
account of the actual condition of the agricultural
labourer from one end of the kingdom to the other.
The pity was that, having secured these admirable
reports, the commissioners failed to utilise them as
briefs on which to examine their authors and other
experts on the subject, so as to elucidate the conclusions, and test the particulars, especially with
regard to the points on which the assistant commissioners differed. Here, indeed, oral evidence would
have been of the utmost value.

But it would be unfair to estimate the relative
evidential value of the spoken and the written word
from the experience of one royal commission only.
The difficulty of giving the case in favour of oral
evidence lies in the paradoxical fact that, exactly
in those instances in which it shows the biggest
yield, there are seldom traces in the published proceedings of the extent to which this method has
been resorted to. We recall the official enquiry in

which, as a member, one of us learnt most from the spoken word—the Machinery of Government Committee, a sub-committee of the Reconstruction Committee of 1917–19. This sub-committee consisted of half a dozen members, including two experienced and remarkably able civil servants, and it was presided over by Lord Haldane. In this case the members were provided, at the outset, with detailed descriptions of the constitution and working of each Government department. Furnished with these confidential memoranda, they enjoyed the privilege of long confidential talks, not only with the officials who had prepared or endorsed them, but also with the officials of other departments, with Cabinet and ex-Cabinet ministers, and with persons having transactions with these departments. By these consultations they were able to test, to correct, and to supplement the written information. In the ease and comfort of a private house, sanctified by the portraits of philosophers and jurists, exhilarated by tea and soothed by tobacco, all sorts of interesting sidelights emerged from this friendly clash of official minds, illuminating the working of particular departments (notably other people's departments) and revealing the relations, "extensive and peculiar", habitual or occasional, between the Cabinet, Parliament, the Civil Service, and the Press. The drawback to this method of taking evidence is that the yield is monopolised by the privileged investigators and cannot be communicated to the public, except in so far as official discretion and political expediency permitted it to appear in a veiled fashion in the descriptions and recommendations included in the final report.[1]

There must be many other instances that could be given of the value of oral evidence when taken under right conditions. But it is significant that, judging from our own experience in social investigation, success is reached under exactly opposite conditions from those prescribed in a court of justice. The first and foremost of these conditions is that the person examined should feel assured of secrecy, and that no word will be published, or even taken down in shorthand, without his specific consent. The other condition, and one we should like to emphasise, is that the witness must be previously furnished with all the relevant reports and statements of fact, and that the oral discussion should in the main proceed on the facts described by these written words.

Can we now sum up the reasons why the experience of a social investigator contradicts the axiom of a court of justice, that the spoken word is of superior evidential value to the written? All the conditions usually present in the taking of evidence by official committees and commissions of enquiry are adverse to the extraction of the truth. The majority of the members of these bodies are neither expert lawyers acquainted with the laws of evidence nor practised social investigators versed in the difficult art of interviewing. Neither the assumed "open

[1] Report of Sub-Committee of the Reconstruction Committee on the Machinery of Government, Cmd. 1919.

mind" of the distinguished personage who is un-
acquainted with the subject to be investigated, nor
the specialised and inside knowledge of the representative of some interest or undertaking involved
in the enquiry, is any kind of substitute for the
special training of the professional lawyer or that
of the sociologist. We may remark incidentally that
we always rejoice to find lawyers on a committee
of which either of us is a member; even an inferior
lawyer being, in our experience, a better instrument
for an oral enquiry than the most distinguished intellectual who is not a practitioner in the art of
eliciting facts from spoken words. Our experience
on Government committees and commissions of
enquiry has, in fact, completely converted us to the
necessity, in modern life, of a highly organised legal
profession. We shudder to think what would happen
in a court of justice if it were deprived of the professional lawyer as solicitor, advocate, and judge.
The second obstacle to the discovery of truth
through oral evidence is the absence, in the majority
of these bodies, of any intelligent procedure. The
selection of witnesses leaves much to be desired, as
this is usually decided by the chairman and secretary, neither of them trained for the task, supplemented by stray suggestions from such of the
members as are interested in bringing forward a
particular set of facts or point of view. Further,
the members of the committee are seldom provided
with any adequate brief specifying the facts which
each witness is competent to prove from his own

knowledge; in some cases, indeed, the witnesses are not even required to hand in written statements for circulation detailing the facts about which they are prepared to be cross-examined. Whether or not an oath be administered to tell "the truth, the whole truth, and nothing but the truth," seems immaterial, as neither the life and liberty, nor the property, of any individual is at stake, and as no penal consequences will follow for anyone concerned (except, by the way, a possible action for libel), a nervous or unscrupulous witness does not trouble himself much about the literal accuracy of his answers. Slowness of wits or the itch of vanity, servility or cantankerousness, the impulse to please or to contradict, will lead a witness to tell little lies, or, at least, to indulge in "terminological inaccuracies", which he would not write down deliberately at his leisure in the solitude of his study or office. In the case of an intentional and artistic liar, the written statement is much better material to dissect for the presence of lies than the spoken word, which can always be withdrawn, altered, or qualified. We may add, incidentally, that proofs of the stenographer's notes are submitted to questioner and witness; and substantial and material alterations can be and are made by both parties—a practice open to abuse. But however cool-headed and scrupulous a witness may be, once in the witness chair he finds himself constantly thrown off the track and prevented from concentrating his mind on telling exactly what he knows and no more than he knows. He may be irritated or bored by elementary questions, the answers to which can be found in any text-book, and ought to be known to any educated person who presumes to take part in the enquiry. Moreover, the witness is not protected by the rules of the court, or by the intervention of the judge or his counsel, from being asked improper or irrelevant questions. He may be cross-examined about some technical detail about which he has no personal knowledge, and upon which he did not expect to be questioned. He may be asked "his opinion" about large masses of statistics, or about problems of administration which he has not considered; and, worst of all, he may be heckled on some abstract theory that he has never thought about. One of us remembers at a sitting of the Royal Commission on the Poor Law, causing a succession of witnesses to give opinions as to what would happen in a series of hypothetical cases in an exactly contrary sense from the answers given by them a few minutes previously when questioned by a colleague. Presently this colleague complained of "Mrs. Webb's unfair cross-examination", to which it was retorted that, as neither commissioner nor the witness was acquainted with the facts—the subjects being the bearing of the "law of rent" on the incidence of rating, and of compounding for rates on the electors' desire for public expenditure—it was hardly worth while to spend public money at the rate of £50 a day in order to "put on the notes" our respective social prejudices. But, apart from this silly dialectic, there are, in this oral evidence before committees of enquiry, usually two fatal defects. "What in your opinion are the relative results of piece-work and time-work on output?" or "What in your opinion are the advantages of voluntary association over governmental organisation?" are common types of question: the answers to them being necessarily as indefinite and as vague as the questions themselves. What seems to be the aim of the keenest members of these committees of enquiry is to get some particular opinion "on the notes", so that they can use it to back up their side in the eventual report. Even when the questioner asks the witness about a particular occurrence within the witness's own knowledge, no attempt is made to check the accuracy of the statement of fact embodied in the answer, by requiring the production of the relevant documents (such as minutes of proceedings, accounts, wages books, etc.), or by getting the testimony of another witness of the same occurrence having a different bias. There is, in short, no verification. Every statement by every witness, whatever his qualifications, is accepted as of equal value and enshrined in the blue-book, thus gaining a quite fictitious evidential value for future generations of students. To put it shortly, the great mass of oral "evidence" given before committees of enquiry relates to opinions on general questions, and not to actual occurrences, whilst even the modicum of fact given in evidence is not checked or verified by other enquiries.

This harsh criticism of the value of the oral evidence given before royal commissions and select and departmental committees is not intended as any depreciation of the general value of these social institutions. It is a very bad royal commission that relies entirely, or even mainly, on oral evidence. Many of the most successful of these bodies—for instance, the great Poor Law and Municipal Corporation Commissions of 1833–35, have relied mainly on the detailed investigations of assistant commissioners, presented in written reports; and their error lay in not taking oral evidence upon these reports from their authors, and from others. In a few cases, the members of the commission themselves go investigating, and their personal experiences are illuminating. Most commissions, moreover, get compiled additional statistics bearing on their subject. Perhaps the most useful of all the services rendered to sociology by these official enquiries is the collection that they usually make, and sometimes publish, of contemporary documents not otherwise accessible to the student. Taken as a whole the massive array of British blue-books stands pre-eminent as a source of information about contemporary social conditions and contemporary public opinion, whilst some of the final reports are, in their constructive relation to legislative and executive activities, great state papers. It must also be remembered that these bodies are seldom designed for scientific research; they are primarily political organs, with political objects. The comment of the cynic that they are created "to shelve a question" is usually unfair: a more favourable expression of the same fact is that they are frequently set up as a safety valve, or as a channel for current agitations and counter agitations, so as to enable the Government, Parliament, and public opinion to test the value of, and to estimate the force behind each of these agitations. From the standpoint of democratic control, and the education of public opinion, the British royal commission or committee of enquiry is the analogue of the American practice of public hearings, at which the representatives of interests and causes, as well as individual cranks and persons with grievances may give utterance to their ideas and their feelings. Finally, many royal commissions and select committees have for their purpose, not enquiry at all as to the facts of social organisation, not even publicity for rival projects or individual grievances, but the hammering out of some practical compromise between contending experts and interests, all of whom are possessed of the necessary data, a compromise eventually embodied in a statute or departmental order.

CHAPTER VIII

WATCHING THE INSTITUTION AT WORK

An indispensable part of the study of any social institution, wherever this can be obtained, is deliberate and sustained personal observation of its actual operation. Though the social institution itself may be, in its wholeness, as invisible and as intangible as the biologist's species, yet the units, items, parts, or particular manifestations of the institution will often be open, under one excuse or another, to close and prolonged inspection, from which the investigator may learn a lot. He clarifies his ideas, which gain in precision and discrimination. He revises his provisional classifications, and tests his tentative hypotheses. What is even more important, the student silently watching a town council or a trade union committee at work, or looking on at a conference of politicians or educationists, picks up hints that help him to new hypotheses, to be, in their turn, tried on other manifestations of his subject-matter.

The trouble about this method of personal observation in the case of social institutions is that the investigator, not being himself a member, can seldom get within sight or hearing of the confidential or intimate proceedings of the institution that he is investigating. On the other hand, it is rarely the case that the members themselves include even one who cares (or is competent) to take a detached or scientific view of what is going on, still less to make it a matter of immediate and accurate record, and to impart such a record to even the friendliest outsider. But there are valuable opportunities of personal observation to be obtained by the resourceful and pertinacious investigator, even if these have to be limited to the public sessions of corporate bodies, civil administrators, and judicial personages. Occasionally the favour of private introduction may give the student a glimpse behind the scenes. This, however, has the drawback that the introduction of a stranger nearly always has the result of seriously altering the proceedings, thus rendering the occasion more or less untypical. There are, of course, many meetings and proceedings to which access is denied to all outsiders. This is particularly the case with profit-making enterprise in the capitalist system.[1] Few and far between are the investigators

---

[1] We remember Professor Graham Wallas telling us, years ago, of a student who imparted to him in confidence that he had become engaged to the daughter of a manufacturer who insisted that his prospective son-in-law should enter his business as a partner. The zealous student deplored that his career as a social investigator would thereby be summarily ended. But Professor Wallas expatiated on the magnificent opportunity for investigation that was opening before him.

"Go into the business," he said, "and incidentally make a fortune. But note down everything relating to the enterprise, keeping precise and voluminous notes of every detail, elucidating them by every fact relating to the industry as a whole, in all its varied reactions—the mass of notes

who can, in the course of their studies, become themselves manufacturers or merchants, stockbrokers or bankers, church dignitaries or ambassadors, town councillors, members of Parliament, highly placed civil servants or ministers of state! The published biographies, reminiscences, and memoirs of such persons should, of course, be consulted, for such scraps of relevant information as they may contain.

We have made a practice of visiting and watching every accessible meeting forming part of the particular social institution that we were studying, from parish councils to parliaments. In the earliest stages of our enquiry we had to learn how to combine the two distinct methods of using the Spoken Word, the interview (in which the investigator is an active agent), and the process of passive attention to words spoken in the course of the business activities of the organisation under examination.

"Exactly three weeks" (it is recorded in the diary under 9th February 1892) "since I settled in Manchester. Have been hard at work looking through minute books, interviewing trade unionists and attending business meetings of trade unions. Extraordinarily stupid of me not to have thought of this idea before: one learns so much more by listening to business being done than by reading the minutes. But it never struck me that I could get into the executive meetings of societies, and observe for my-

being eventually worked up into such a scientific monograph on profit-making enterprises as the world has never yet possessed."

Unfortunately, though the course of true love ran smoothly, that scientific monograph was never written!

self the sort of questions which arise. . . . At present
it is difficult to see the wood for the trees. I am grop-
ing about, holding on to one trunk after another,
trying to follow the direction of its roots, and the
lines of growth of its branches, and getting sadly
mixed up between one species and another. . . . The
publication of my engagement to S. W. (I find
myself noting with satisfaction) has not injured me
in the very least, except perhaps with Birtwhistle
(the Conservative general secretary of the Cotton
Weavers)."

Four months later one of the authors was at Leeds
attending the delegate meeting of the great Amalgamated Society of Engineers (now the Amalgamated
Engineering Union); whilst a secretary, duly instructed in our methods, was interviewing, in succession, such of the sixty-eight delegates as were
accessible. The following entries in the diary will
enable the student to realise the general impressions
and out-of-the-way details gathered in by this process of "watching the organisation at work":

"Leeds. July 2nd, 1892. Interesting time at Leeds.
Engineers' delegate meeting to revise rules, to which
I have been admitted by special resolution. The
sixty-eight delegates sit for six hours a day. This
meeting will be a crisis in the history of the A.S.E.
For some time past, under the guidance of a weak
secretary, there has been trouble within and without. The spirit and aspirations of the New Unionism
have infected even this conservative and aristocratic
body, which until a few years ago was little better

than a great benefit society. Not that the A.S.E. has
not fought its battles in the past. The Nine Hours
Movement 1872 was the beginning of a great revival
of Trade Unionism and was initiated by members of
the A.S.E. But except for one or two pitched battles
at long intervals, the routine of benefit claims has
been uninterrupted and the A.S.E. has appeared to
its members, in the remotest districts of the country,
simply as one more great friendly society for mutual
help in common needs.

"The scene has changed during the last two years.
The two foremost figures in the Labour World, Tom
Mann and John Burns, happen to belong to the
A.S.E. Though they won their reputations in organising unskilled workers, and in the politico-
socialist movement, yet their fellow-members became proud of them and have been greatly influenced
by their powerful cry of 'forward'. In the larger
districts, and especially on the North-East coast,
the A.S.E. have been stimulated to strike for new
'privileges'. This has led to serious friction between
the local district authorities with a definite trade
policy, and the central and unrepresentative executive in London, fitted, by its constitution, only to
administer a friendly society.[1] No guidance and no

---

[1] In Mr. F. W. Galton's notes of interviews deposited at the London
School of Economics in the Webb Collection of Trade Union Documents
will be found the transition from the method of the Questionnaire and
analytic note-taking. For instance, in the long series of interviews with
the officials of the forty odd Sheffield cutlery trade unions, Mr. Galton
discards our questions and gives all the facts elicited under such general
headings as Methods of Remuneration, Hours of Labour, Constitution,
etc. Unfortunately these notes were not kept on separate sheets of paper
for each heading; the consequence was that when we required informa-

control, and yet an irritating repudiation or a dilatory acceptance of the already acted on decisions of the local district committees, have brought the London Council into universal disrepute. And to make confusion worse confounded, the elaborate and complicated local organisation—branch committees, local district committees, central district committees, grand committees, and joint committees—has resulted in a mass of divergent policies presented by these different centres of authority, irritating alike to the members and to the employers, and entailing public discredit and dissatisfaction and discord among the members.

"The recent disasters on the North-East coast have ripened discontent into a resolution to change fundamentally the constitution of the society. Hence last year the members voted, by a large majority, for a delegate meeting (the last was in 1885). For the past six months revision committees have been sitting in all the centres of the engineering industry. The result is a book of suggestions, 258 pages of closely printed amendments to the present rules, emanating from all parts of the United Kingdom, and even from America and Australasia. The delegates are confined to these suggestions: they cannot propose any amendment which does not appear in the book.

tion on all the separate points of constitution and structure for our analytic description of the trade union world, we had to ask Mr. Galton to take out of all the notes the information embodied in them in a necessarily abstracted form, instead of having the full information recorded in the original note at our disposal by reshuffling the sheets.

"The general trend of the suggestions are: first, in favour of more local government; secondly, in favour of more salaried officials; thirdly, in favour of a representative executive council, instead of a governing branch or district as heretofore; and fourthly, a widening of the basis of the membership by the admission of other classes. The first proposal, or set of proposals, are fraught with difficulty; and I think if they were to be adopted in any of the proposed forms the A.S.E. would be doomed. There is no suggestion to decentralise the finance. Should more freedom be given to districts, the funds of the whole society would be liable to pay for the action of any district. These proposals altogether overlook the fundamental principle that the power to govern and to tax must be in the same hands. It would be as if Leeds could draw unlimited amounts from the national exchequer in order to build water works or buy parks, without incurring any financial responsibility. Put in this way the harder-headed of the delegates, though pledged to support the proposals, saw the objection clearly enough. These proposals have not yet come before the meeting, but I gather that they will not be very seriously entertained.

"The second and third suggestions: the appointment of more salaried officers and the alteration of the constitution of the executive council, have been combined in a proposal to constitute a permanent executive council representing eight electoral districts. This proposal has been carried and incorporated in the rules. I listened to a six hours debate upon the subject; one of the most level-headed discussions I have ever heard. There are half a dozen delegates who are quite admirable debaters, clear, forcible and concise. The language and arrangement of some of the speeches is excellent, and makes one wish to see the speakers in Parliament. There is no limit of time, but this freedom to prose or rant has not been abused; and I listened for six hours with no sense of boredom or impatience. My notes will give the gist of the arguments on both sides.

"The last fundamental change proposed, the widening of the basis of the society, that is, the admission of other classes, was brought forward as the first business. This proposal, or rather proposals (for there were some ten classes of workers suggested by revision committees to be included), is only the last of a series of changes which have been made in the constitution of the A.S.E. during the forty years of its existence. It began by being a society of highly skilled mechanics; then the members saw fit to include skilled machinists. At this delegate meeting they have gone a step further and offer to cater for skilled labourers, besides admitting all kinds of small specialised groups of men who belong to engineering establishments. It was even suggested that they should offer to take in plumbers and iron-moulders, two sections already provided for by old and flourishing unions. It is possible that this policy of inclusion has been forced on the A.S.E. through the continuous difficulty of overlapping and apportionment, together with the substitution of one class of workers for another, a process which abounds in the engineering and shipbuilding works. But the policy of inclusion has its own dangers. Sectional societies, with strong and consistent policies, or growing rich by inertia, have sprung up on all sides of the great amalgamation, and regard it as their common enemy. Indeed, as recent events on the North-East coast show, it seems likely that there will be a tacit union of all these sectional societies to checkmate and arrest the growth of the A.S.E. It is pathetic to watch the delegates trying to find a way out of the dilemma of rival societies competing for the same class of workers. A vague longing for one great amalgamation forces them into an antagonistic policy towards sectional societies. More especially were they bitter against the United Kingdom Society of Patternmakers.

"The conference is more or less divided up into sections or caucuses, pledged to certain definite programmes of reform, though, on the whole, there is a *bona fide* discussion of all the proposals. London and the North-East coast have sent the 'Forward' party, and their delegates are generally found voting for the policy of inclusion and efficiency. Manchester and Lancashire generally represent a solid conservative reactionary vote, and have opposed any radical change. Scotland would follow suit if it were not for a certain Home Rule tendency. Belfast is ultra-Tory and has one fixed idea: restriction and exclusion. The Midland delegates as well as the Yorkshire scatter their votes indiscriminately between the other sections. But undoubtedly the most level-headed, as well as the ablest speakers, are socialists: for instance, Evans, Brighton; Sellicks, Woolwich; Barnes,[1] Chelsea; Fletcher, Newcastle; Halston, Gateshead. This is altogether an agreeable surprise to me. My experience has been always that the more feather-headed are socialists. But socialism is rapidly changing in character, it is losing its revolutionary tone and note of personal exasperation, and becoming constitutional effort based on hope and not on hatred. The Manchester men, so also the Scottish and the Irish, are for the most part hard-grained individualists. But with the exception of Fergusson of Glasgow, they have no remarkable men among them; and though they show a certain shrewd caution, they are narrow-minded and illiberal. In fact they are not good samples. Whether this is chance, or whether it signifies a general conversion of the more generous hearted and intelligent workmen to socialist economics is a moot question. The socialism is of a decided Fabian type, and one recognises the facts and figures and general arguments taken from Fabian literature."

Another entry in the diary, four years later, describes a visit to another great trade union at work.

"Birmingham. January 15th 1896. Came here last night on receipt of telegram from Ashton that I might attend Miners' Federation Annual Conference.

---

[1] George Nicoll Barnes, General Secretary of the A.S.E. from 1900 to 1906, afterwards Labour M.P., 1906-22, member of Mr. Lloyd George's Cabinets from 1917 to 1922.

This assembly rules the Miners' Federation. It consists of about forty delegates, each county sending as many representatives as it thinks fit, and electing them as it thinks fit. As the voting on all important issues is by cards—*i.e.* according to the number of men represented—there is no object in sending more than will express the views of the constituents. All the Miners' Agents are present and have with them, as colleagues, a certain number of representative men, either checkweighmen or working miners. The agenda is prepared by the executive. Each county has the right to send propositions to be considered. But apparently the executive (composed exclusively of salaried officials) decides what propositions shall be submitted, and how they shall be grouped or placed, and uses its power with considerable vigour. It depends on the official or officials who represent a given county on the executive committee whether a county recommendation is or is not placed on the agenda. These officials dominate the conference. If the representatives of a county find themselves forced to bring forward a proposal against their better judgment, they can always depend on the officials of the other counties quietly to dismiss it. No business except that on the agenda may be discussed until the agenda is disposed of; and even then it can only be discussed 'academically'—it cannot be decided on.

"So much for the constitution. The conference was held in a third-rate hotel. When I arrived at 10 A.M. punctually, I found a little group of Miners'

Agents at the entrance and they took me through
the bar and up the stairs to a long, narrow room,
somewhat ill-lighted and ventilated, with two rows
of tables already littered with Agenda papers, drafts
of the Coal Mines Regulation Bill, and the verbatim
report of Pickard's opening speech. Already some
twenty men were lounging in the room, and the re-
porters were settling themselves down at the table.
I was seated beside Pickard, the President; on the
other side of me Bailey of Nottingham. Pickard
opened the proceedings by an attack on the *Birmingham Post*, or as he puts it—the Birmingham past
(that is the sort of humour indulged in)—for its
comments on his opening address delivered the day
before. He is a disagreeable person—suspicious, irri-
table, autocratic—his best characteristic being a
pig-headed persistency in sticking to certain principles such as 'wages ruling prices' and a 'legal day'.
He is an extreme party Liberal, and both in his opening address and in his rejoinder to the press this
morning, he denounced the Tories and all their
works. Indeed, under his inspiration all the speakers,
nearly all of them officials, showed party feeling and
extreme enmity against Chamberlain, which was not
wise proceeding in face of five years Tory Government. The debate was purely formal. It consisted of
a series of set speeches in favour of employers' liability (without contracting out), and eight hours
without local option. Everybody was agreed, and
the speeches were made with a view of impressing
the press, and had the full flavoured rhetoric and

comic stories of platform orations. This prearranged display bored the delegates, and one after another they quietly slipped out for a smoke or a 'liquor up'. The unreality of the whole business was relieved by a deputation from the National Enginemen's Association asking the Federation to save them from the local option proposed by Durham; the three or four hundred members in Durham insisting on their right, as a minority, of opting themselves out of local option!

"Very different was the discussion in the afternoon. From this meeting the press were excluded. All the rhetoric and the little well-known comic tales were dropped; all allusions to the 'aims and aspirations' of the working class and all references to the House of Lords and 'tyrant capitalists' vanished. The amendments proposed to the bill as now printed were discussed in a strictly practical manner. Harvey, the Derbyshire Agent, brought up the proposal that the working miners, instead of being permitted to appoint one among themselves to inspect the mine, should be compelled to do so by altering 'may' into 'shall'. It was obvious from his speech that he did not believe in the proposal; but he gave the best argument for it by asserting that so long as the clause was only permissive the men who examined the mines were victimised. If it was compulsory employers would accept the examination, and therefore the examiner. No sooner had he sat down than up rose five or six delegates to speak against the suggestion on the ground that it was either impracticable or inexpedient. The conference was of two minds as to the desirability of increasing the responsibility of the men for the safety of the mine. 'All our past legislation', declared Bailey, 'has been in the direction of throwing the onus of inspection on the state, and the onus of responsibility for the condition of the mines on the employers. If you insist on forcing the men to inspect the mines through their representative once a month, this inspection will be used against you in case of accident.' But the more constant note was the impracticability. 'You cannot make a coward into a man by Act of Parliament', thundered old Cowie. 'If the pit refuses to appoint examiners, will you summon the whole lot of them? And how can you prevent their examiner from giving a false report in order to please the employer?' In the end the proposal was dismissed by card vote: 144 to 20.

"Another amendment proposed by Derbyshire, brought up the vexed question of what is a 'practical man'. Derbyshire proposed that no man should be appointed deputy who had not worked five years at the face. Cowie again interposed with the apt remark that a man might be an experienced coal-getter and yet might know nothing about ventilation, or mine management. An examination as test of competency and five years working in the mine, substituted for five years working at the face, was accepted. A proposed prohibition of the butty system was adjourned until to-morrow. Pickard makes an indifferent chairman. He is good at keeping order, but never sees the point, and is oddly muddle-headed. . . .

"July 16. Sitting for five or six hours in a stinking room, with an open sewer on one side and ill-ventilated urinals on the other, is not an invigorating occupation. But in spite of headache and mental depression I am glad I came. These two days debate have made me better appreciate the sagacity, good-temper and fair-mindedness of these miners than I could have done by reading endless reports. Their speeches, to which by the way there is no time-limit, are admirable: clear and to the point; and show a thorough grip of the subject. Of course, the whole debate turned on minute technical points, exactly the questions which these officials are always dealing with, and with which they are therefore thoroughly familiar. No. 5 on the agenda, the proposal to penalise the butty system, was withdrawn, owing to the delegate from Staffordshire maintaining that many of his members were contractors, and that he therefore begged for another adjournment. Another proposition, from Derbyshire (No. 6), which Harvey moved with the laconic remark that he had no opinion about it, a proposition insisting on the use of an automatic weighing machine. On this a very detailed and technical discussion arose. Yorkshire delegates against proposal, on the ground that what was needed was additional checkweighmen, and perhaps additional weighing machines; some of the automatic machines were worse than the beam machine, were more often out of order than in order. Then Bailey of Nottingham arose, and in a perfectly clear speech explained the exact position. Undoubtedly a self-registering machine was the best for the men. Under the beam machine the company's weighman, under compulsion from the company, was always cheating the men of a quarter here and quarter there; and when the output was large and the tubs had to be hurried through, it was more than the men's checkweighman could do, to prevent unfair handling. With a self-registering machine this could not happen, unless the company were prepared to falsify the machine, which would be difficult and risky. But if a self-registering machine were used you must have a solid pit mouth; if there was vibration the machine would get out of order. The general feeling was on the whole against the proposed amendment, on the ground that there were so many different automatic machines, and some were very bad. Moreover, there were exceptional mines in which it would be difficult to keep any such machine in working order. The previous question passed. No. 7 moved by Yorkshire. A very insidious proposal from the employers' point of view: a clause to be inserted to permit the election of an assistant checkweighman 'whenever the checkweighman is acting *in any other capacity* for or on behalf of the workmen of such colliery'. As Parrott remarked: 'it was very convenient to use the checkweighman for "association business"'; the election of an assistant would enable the checkweighman to go off for the day to arrange a dispute. Seeing that the checkweighman is paid by a compulsory levy on all the men in a mine (should the majority decide to have one) this proposal was acceptable to a meeting of trade unionists. Agreed to. Three other propositions came up and were passed almost without discussion. The only fight was on the Scottish business. The Scottish Federation had sent forward various resolutions to be submitted to the conference. One of them, proposing a technical alteration in the clause regulating deductions, was ruled out by the executive. It was apparently a proposal which the Scottish Federation had already tried to get into Asquith's Bill, and to which the English miners strongly objected. At first Pickard declared that the resolution had not been received in time. But afterwards it was admitted, both by Wood and Ashton, that the executive had had it before them, but had used their discretion and not inserted it in the agenda; Scottish delegates protested: Who gave the executive that power? Wanted to move the suspension of standing orders to discuss this constitutional question. 'It has been the custom', persisted Pickard, 'for the executive committee to draw up the agenda; if you want to alter the rule you must give notice before the next conference. We shall not refuse to place the proposal to alter the rule on the agenda, because it would be virtually a vote of censure on us. But I am not going to have it discussed without notice. No Trades Union Congress for me!' Again the Scottish brought forward No. 16 on the programme: an attempt to prevent the English miners from concluding an agreement with their employers, unless such agreement extended to Scotland. On this resolution the Scottish were divided among themselves—Weir, the Fife Agent, stating with dignity and decision that he really did not think the English could be expected to accept such a suggestion. Pickard promised that the Scottish delegates should have an opportunity of raising the question at the special conference which would be summoned before a new agreement was come to by the English miners and their employers. This ended the proposed amendments to the Mines Regulation Amendment Bill. I was requested to withdraw whilst the conference discussed the auditor's report—the miners are very secretive about their balance sheet! No question of wages or collective bargaining has come up. Apparently Pickard and the executive committee decided to rule the wages question out of the agenda, in spite of the fact that several districts had sent formal resolutions to be considered for an advance of wages. 'Better let sleeping dogs lie,' Pickard repeated again and again when the question of wages was referred to. . . .

"July 17th. A morning sitting terminated the proceedings—the election of the executive committee of eleven officials. Each large district puts forward its own men, and all the large districts vote for each other's candidates. There is one place on the committee which is deliberately left open for the smaller districts (such as North Wales, Cleveland, South Derbyshire) to fight for, the delegates of Lancashire and Yorkshire casting their vote in rotation for one or other of them. The constitution of the executive committee is therefore little altered year by year, except that when a district has a good many officials all of whom like serving, they take it turn and turn about to be 'put up' for the Federation executive committee. Representatives to be sent to other congresses are elected more haphazard. But there is a general sense of fair play; giving every district and every man his due. The sense of 'fair-play' is perhaps the most remarkable feature in these working-class organisations; there is an extraordinary absence of personal spite or intolerance. This amounts almost to a fault; they sacrifice efficiency and intellectual conviction to this over-powering instinct for 'equal treatment'.

"After the election was over, Harvey rose in his seat and asked whether he might raise the 'wages question'. It had, he said, been ruled out of the agenda, but he proposed, now that the business was finished, to bring the resolution sent up by Derbyshire before the meeting. Pickard promptly replied that he should 'rule it out of order', whereupon Harvey collapsed with a broad grin. The responsible officials were obviously glad to be saved any discussion of the subject. Pickard encouraged the meeting to discuss the International Miners' Congress, and talked at length about the unbusinesslike conduct of the foreigners; but allowed the conference to instruct him to take steps to call an International Conference this year. It is almost impossible to understand why Pickard is allowed to rule with such a high hand, unless it is because he is a bully, holds himself aloof, and knows his own mind. To look at he is an ugly surly brute, with small suspicious eyes, an unwieldly corporation, red face and unpleasant manner; a cross between a bulldog and a pig. I rather expected they would ask me to say a few words, but Pickard evidently did not intend to, so I shook hands cordially with him, and left just after the vote of thanks to the chairman. I hurried back to the hotel; packed up and left by the first train from that damnable Birmingham for my own dear little home. Found Sidney only too glad to get me back. . . .

"Thinking back on the conference there were not many interesting personalities. Cowie, the Yorkshire giant, for twenty years checkweighman, now holding some nominal post in the Yorkshire Society, but acting as the representative of the Miners at Congresses and on the Parliamentary Committee (of the Trades Union Congress). A single-minded, upright man, with vigorous racy phraseology, a gift of eloquence, and a stertorous voice, which he likes to listen to. Distinctly the representative, and not the official. Ashton (secretary to the Federation), a mild, blue-eyed, light-bearded Lancashire man, slow of speech, somewhat stupid, with a dog-like fidelity to the Federation, and abject loyalty to Pickard. He also is without guile, with a deep-rooted respect for his betters, and with the quiet dignity of a hard-working and unobtrusive man who has won his way by sheer honesty. Sam Woods (Vice-President) has the appearance of a dapper dissenting minister, with endless self-complacency, remarkable fluency, a pleasant voice and somewhat servile manner, trying to please all persons; in politics a mere booby. Parrott of Yorkshire is a typical official, looks like a respectable bank clerk, seldom speaks, but when he does shows sense and determination, and a self-restrained dislike of Pickard. Harvey of Derbyshire, Bailey of Nottingham, Stanley of Cannock Chase, all of them excellent speakers. The charmingly refined Scotsman, Weir, secretary of the Fife Miners; tall, good looking, with a melancholy expression and slow speech and gentle ways. When one comes to think of it, Pickard rules because he is the only really strong personality, the only man with a sufficiently big ambition. Many of these men are vain; but few have a persistent desire to push themselves into positions of authority. Above all, though they abound in common sense, they have very little initiative, their very self-complacency is of a passive character. Revolution to these men would be impossible; step by step reform is difficult (except with regard to their own trade), and they are, barring a traditional radicalism, intensely conservative and slow to move or convince."

When we turned from Trade Unionism to English Local Government, as the subject to be investigated, the opportunities for "watching the institution at work" were as manifold as they were suggestive. One of us, for instance, went to the other end of England to attend a Local Government Board public inquiry into an application for an extension of borough boundaries. We append a diary entry in which the procedure is described:

"Three days sitting in bad atmosphere listening to the argument whether or not —— and —— shall be included in the borough of ——. I had an introduction from —— of the L.G.B. to the Inspector who was holding the enquiry, one General ——; and I happened to light on the hotel where two of the leading counsel engaged in the case were staying. Unfortunately, the hotel was small and crowded, so that there was not much opportunity for confidential talks with judge and counsel; and the local men were too flustered to give me much information. But I quickly made friends with three out of the five counsel—X—, Y—, and Z—. General —— is a gouty and slow-minded old West-End club-man, past his work even if he were ever capable of it— the relic, I imagine, of the era of barefaced jobbery of appointments. I am not impressed with the quality of the legal ability present at the enquiry. Perhaps these extension cases do not lend themselves to a careful mustering of proven facts or to subtlety of argument. Hearsay evidence as to the wishes of this or that section of the population and jumbles of irrelevant considerations, the reiteration of stock arguments for or against extensions of boundaries in general—such as 'larger areas mean more efficient administration' or 'smaller areas are more conducive to keen interest', that a particular district is or is not the outgrowth of an older in-habited area, that borough government is more

desirable than that of an urban district council, that
the amenities of the borough are or are not shared
with the surrounding districts—I felt that I could
have reeled it all off mechanically if I had just been
told on which side I was to plead. As to the evidence,
it was all of the nature of personal opinions, obviously *ex parte* opinions; no attempt was made to
prove the truth or the falsehood of all this assertion,
and counter assertion. Then there is the silly badger-
ing of inexperienced witnesses. 'Will you answer yes
or no, Mr. Jones,' when, in the opinion of the nervous witness, 'yes' would be misleading and 'no' inaccurate. It was easy to see that any facts obtained
and many not obtained by this expensive process
could have been got by a -couple of experienced
investigators examining witnesses quietly in their
homes as well as documents which had not been
faked for the occasion. X— and Z— lent me their
briefs to read, and it was quite clear to me, as I sat
and listened to the proceedings, that the K.C.'s,
drawing huge fees, had added nothing whatever to
the facts or the arguments prepared for them by the
local solicitor. The culminating absurdity of the proceeding is that if the decision of the L.G.B. Inspector
(who by the way took little or no interest in the talk
of the counsel) is not accepted by the parties concerned, the whole case will have to be argued out
again before a Parliamentary Committee. Personally
I came out of court not having heard one of the
issues raised adequately cleared up—certainly not
the general issue of larger or smaller areas of adminis-

tration. At present I am divided in my mind between the desirability of large municipal boroughs and the expediency of keeping alive the old historic county, and therefore the minor local authorities under county jurisdiction. . . ."[1]

We give a few more entries, by one or other of us, descriptive of American government during our stay in the United States in the spring of 1898:

"Last night I attended the meeting of the City Council, the lower chamber of the municipal legislature (of Boston, Mass.).

"The Council was the lowest depth in representative bodies that we have yet explored. Its powers are limited practically to concurring with the Aldermen in voting the appropriations. It has no patronage and was until lately not paid. The members then gave themselves carriage-rides and dinners, so now they get £60 a year ($300) in lieu. It is an assembly of 75 members, elected three each by 25 wards; 42 were Democrat and 33 Republican. The position is evidently despised, not only by the good citizen, but even by the ward politician of any standing, for half the members were youths between 20 and 35, striplings describing themselves as law students, medical students, clerks, telegraphists, stenographers, with half a dozen bar-tenders and billiard markers. The president was a short, slight stripling of 30. I saw only one man of 50 among the whole 75. There were two young negroes (law students), two Russian Jews (very sensible men, small dealers), and about

[1] MS. Diary, 3rd February 1900.

thirty Irish—three different Donovans for instance. There were car-drivers, hackmen, labourers and mechanics; a few little grocers, a peddlar or two— the whole forming the queerest debating society kind of legislative body I ever saw. But the council had a *beauté de diable*—these young men, with the cleanest of collars and cuffs, and nice jacket suits, had a distinctly more pleasing appearance than the flashy, overfed, dissipated ward politicians of the New York and Philadelphia Councils. What they most resembled was the debating society of a London Polytechnic Institute.

"The same crude and imperfect procedure; forms identical with those of Congress, as also the arrangement of the chamber, the president on his raised dais and square table, with clerks below him, and all the paraphernalia of officials around him. This body costs Boston, in stipends alone, for members and officials, over £8000 a year, and is worth less than nothing. The procedure of the 'motion to reconsider' seems to amount usually to this: that after every resolution passed, one of the members 'moves to reconsider'; the president announces that 'Mr. Jones moves reconsideration, hoping the same will not prevail!' It is then formally put and negatived. This prevents anyone else moving 'to reconsider', as he otherwise could at the next meeting; and so makes the vote conclusive.

"The principal business was to pass a vote for $300,000 for street and other improvements, submitted in a lump sum by the executive, without details: no one asked for details, but it was moved and carried by 35 to 32 that, instead of a lump sum of $300,000, $16,000 be spent in each of the 25 wards. It was in vain pointed out that this was wasteful and absurd, as the need and size of improvements differed. However, it was freely said in debate that neither the Aldermen nor the Mayor would agree, so that the evening was wasted on a purely academic discussion. . . ."[1]

"Baltimore: The Mayor was an immense man like some strange animal . . . has been in office some months and says most of his time has been taken up in making the new appointments. He was returned by the action of the mugwumps who veered round to the Republicans in order to break the Democratic machine which has always ruled the city. (Why is a mugwump like a ferry: because he spends his life in going from side to side.) But he has disappointed the mugwumps by dismissing all the officials and appointing new ones. He told us that he could not avoid doing so because 'the American is a practical man' and will not go on working for his party, and see other men grow old in office. . . .

"We afterwards attended the meetings of both branches of the council. In both chambers the members were lounging in their seats smoking and dozing or reading newspapers, whilst the president and the clerk transacted the business. Procedure as childish as usual. No printed agenda; all resolutions and bills read word by word by the clerk. The council, con-

[1] MS. Diary, 20th May 1898.

sidering itself a legislature and not an administrative body, reads all ordinances three times and has all sorts of mechanical checks to hasty legislation,which, of course, only operate when the party in power desires the business checked. Bad type of councillor— all ward politicians. The machines of both parties are at present in abeyance, the dominant Republican party being split into sections. Each man is therefore for himself. In the present state of public morality there is no advantage to the community in the absence of a machine and its boss. Though the corporations find this council as a whole more difficult to buy, there is more petty corruption and more inefficiency and blundering than when there is a well-organised machine, with a corporate consciousness of responsibility to the citizens and with a capable man as leader. The boss, who is seldom if ever a member of the council, makes it his business not merely to 'deal' with the large corporations in the interests of his party, but to take counsel with able business men as to how the financial affairs of the city can be best managed. He also vetoes any scandalous appointments. In the large number of transactions in which he cannot benefit his party by selling the interests of the city, he is an efficient, well-informed, and comparatively long-sighted administrator, susceptible to public opinion and newspaper criticism.

"Philadelphia: The city government is a hotbed of corruption, though according to Talcott Williams (our host, then editor of the *Philadelphia Press*) it is improving. . . . There is no party strife in the council; the Republican party being overwhelmingly strong. But certain members are known to 'belong' to this or that powerful corporation or to this or that boss. We attended a session of each chamber; the members were a low-looking lot. All the same, these ward politicians have a certain distinction of physiognomy: they are forceful men; a strange combination of organising capacity, good fellowship, loose living, shrewdness, and strong will! The corrupt municipal councillor in England is usually undistinguishable from any other ordinary man; if anything he is more commonplace, with less intelligence and less character than his fellows. In the U.S.A. he is a professional, with an expertness, a self-confidence, and a strength of his own. Hence the appearance of these city councils is in a sense more distinguished than one would expect to see in an English town council noted for corrupt dealings; at once more distinguished and more degraded. The well-shaped head and prominent eyes, heavy jaws, self-confident and easy manner, and ready tongue, make many of the ward politicians far more attractive and interesting species of parasites than the seedy little nondescript shamefaced persons who, in English Local Government, happen to be open to corrupt influences."[1]

By way of contrast, we add our account of a conversation with a leading American politician in the lobby of Congress, which revealed to us something that we had been unable to learn from all the serious

[1] MS. Diary, 1898.

studies of the American Constitution, or from its text. On a critical day, when war with Spain was to be decided on, we had been sitting in the gallery of the House of Representatives, listening to the extra-ordinary trivialities by which that body was filling up time. The diary proceeds as follows:

"About 4.30 P.M., after four hours of these inter-estingly irrelevant proceedings, we began to weary, and went down to the Democratic lobby, and sent in our card to B——, leader of the Democrats. Clean-shaven, with large sensual features, long black oily hair and enormous expanse of white shirt, finished off with white evening tie, to English eyes looks a strange combination of a low-class actor and rowdy stump orator. With familiar friendliness and unctuous tones he motioned us into a recess, and enquired what he could do for us. We asked for some explana-tion of the day's proceedings. 'Well, you see, it is just as well to let them talk. We don't want them to pass laws, at least we Democrats don't. We think that there are too many laws already, and that most of them were better repealed. . . .' 'With your usual practical capacity,' I smilingly observe, 'you manage remarkably well; you certainly attain your end with an almost artistic finish. But what, meanwhile, is the Committee on Foreign Relations doing (the Presi-dent's Message on Cuba had been, without debate, formally referred to that Committee on the previous day).' 'Oh,' said he, 'that has been waiting till the Republican majority have settled their internal quarrels. It met yesterday afternoon at four o'clock.

The Republicans adjourned it until 10 the next morning. Then, when the Democrats came this morning, the Republicans again adjourned it until 12 o'clock; then again till 3 o'clock. I hear that this afternoon they presented their resolutions and left the Democrats in the committee room to consider them. The committee will report to-morrow.' 'Do committees never meet then?' I ask. 'No important committee meets as a whole,' answered B——. 'For instance, the committee of Ways and Means, which prepared the new tariff, never considered the tariff. The Republicans took weeks to manufacture it, then laid it before us—I was a member of that committee —and gave us exactly 24 hours to consider it before the committee reported it to the House.' "

Now, we had learned from Woodrow Wilson's *Congressional Government*, on which Lord Bryce had mainly based his account of the constitutional structure, that it was in the committees of the House of Representatives, each directing its own allotted groups of subjects on which legislation was required, that was to be found the analogue, so far as lawmaking was concerned, of the British Cabinet. But Woodrow Wilson, then professor at Princeton University, had worked entirely from the printed documents and the learned literature on the subject, without thinking necessary any personal observation of the institution at work. Clearly, committees which never meet for discussion between opposing parties; which know nothing of the fruitful "give and take" across the table, with demonstration and rebuttal, and are merely alternating party caucuses of majority and minority, are something so different from what Lord Bryce and his English readers understood by "committee government" as to amount to a different species, if not to quite another genus. Our brief conversation with the democratic leader destroyed a whole chapter of faulty generalisation.[1]

RECORDING GENERAL IMPRESSIONS

It is needless to describe in further detail the methods by which, for six solid years, we investigated British Trade Unionism, or the ten years during which we were at work on English Local Government. During these years we spent all the recesses of the London County Council, of which one of us was an active member, in one provincial town after another, first concentrating on Trade Unionism, examining the generally scanty records of the local unions, and collecting books of rules, annual reports, and controversial broadsheets and pamphlets; everywhere interviewing employers and foremen, union officials and members of the rank

[1] We did not fail promptly to verify our observation by enquiries of other Congressmen and finally by going straight to Speaker Read, then the autocrat of the House, by whom the statement was confirmed—and explained as resulting simply from the first principles of Democracy! Why should the minority be consulted: was it not for the majority to decide?

The reader must not assume that the foregoing represents the present practice of the House of Representatives. We understand that, with the subsequent overthrow of the supremacy of the Republican party, and of the autocracy of "Czar Read" as Speaker, considerable changes took place, not only in the method of appointment but also in the practice of the committees of the House. What the "committee system" now amounts to at Washington can be discovered only by personal observation.

and file, and attending the business meetings of trade unions and trades councils. Then, after a tour round the English-speaking world, which we devoted to the working of Democracy generally, we settled down to English Local Government, visiting once more the provincial towns in order to read a couple of centuries of minutes, and to attend council meetings and interview councillors and officials. We mention these local visitations in order to bring in another kind of note, with which we found it useful to supplement the rest of our material. We endeavoured to write, at the end of each of our visits to the principal centres, a rapid summary of our general impression, gained chiefly from the Spoken Word, of the state of organisation in that particular district. These recorded notes of general impressions, either as to particular localities or as to particular phases of the enquiry, are a valuable addition to analytic note-taking. We may conclude with a sample; a survey of the state of trade unionism in and around Glasgow in the autumn of 1892, after a visit of six weeks' duration.

"Glasgow, 1892.—In Glasgow there are a hundred trade unions but there is very little trade unionism. To take, for instance, the engineering and shipbuilding trades, which form the great staple industry of the Clyde, the Boilermakers alone have a really effective union. The A.S.E. is regarded, both by employers and other unions, as a benefit society, and is very little heard of. The Scottish Ironmoulders have a much larger proportion of society men than the A.S.E., but they confine their attempts at trade regulation to the very minimum. The Associated Blacksmiths are powerful, and respected by the employers, but they have not succeeded in obtaining a minimum rate, neither do they regulate piece-work, overtime, or the number of apprentices. The numerous small sectional societies, such as the Iron-grinders (reputed strong), Coppersmiths, Brass-moulders, Brassfinishers, Bolt - makers, etc., are chiefly occupied in maintaining their existence, and in struggling to outwit the A.S.E. in attracting members. Hardly any of these is of five years' standing, and each successive depression of trade scatters their ephemeral organisations to the winds. Black-legging each other's disputes is a very prevalent feature of all the minor societies, whilst the A.S.E. is universally regarded as, in this respect, the common enemy. One's impression is that, outside the ranks of the 'Black Squad' (boilermakers), three-fourths of the men engaged in the engineering and metal trades on the Clyde are non-society men. The shipwrights are in bad odour with the employers, not for aggression but for laziness. They form a compact but inert body, being apparently in process of being squeezed out by the more energetic ship-joiners.

"The lack of energetic organisation on the part of the different trades is shown by the almost complete absence on the Clyde of those disputes about demarcation between trades which are such a feature of the North-East coast.

"The Clyde employers in shipbuilding and engineering appear to be able and independent 'captains of industry', neither, like those on the Tyne, drifting helplessly before the disputes of the unions, nor, like those of Manchester, respected by and respecting the well-established and soberly led trade organisations. Their attitude with regard to all trade questions is one of 'doing what they like with their own'. For instance, piece-work and contracting are, in spite of all the unions, firmly established on the Clyde.

"During the recent years of prosperity, two powerful societies have been formed among the steel-workers. Both the Steel-smelters and the Millmen are engaged in constant disputes to maintain their high piece-work rates in face of improved processes. They have hitherto succeeded in retaining good earnings, rising, in some cases, to extravagant amounts. On the other hand, they have signally failed to reduce their long hours or to abolish Sunday labour. It is worth notice that the members of both these societies, as well as the boilermakers, are, if not 'small masters', at any rate largely interested in squeezing the utmost effort out of subordinate unskilled labour paid by the day. The blast-furnacemen were, it may be noted, completely defeated in their great strike for the abolition of Sunday labour. The Scottish ironstone mines are getting worked out.

"The chief feature in the building trades is the contentment of the societies with the conduct of the employers, and the maintenance of rates in face of a large preponderance of non-society men. This result, which is marked by the fact that non-society men were in all cases reported to receive the same remuneration and privileges as trade unionists, is perhaps accounted for by the rapid growth of Glasgow, and the building operations consequent on railway extensions.

"The textile industries are, in the main, un-organised. Embedded in a mass of female labour, to be counted by tens of thousands, there are half a dozen small and exclusive unions of men engaged in various subsidiary processes, each employing a few hundred persons. These unions have little inter-communication and no common action. They rigorously limit entry into their respective trades, and maintain high rates of remuneration.

"Among other societies, the Compositors and the Tailors are almost the only ones of any considerable standing and exercising control over their trades. Both these are beginning to suffer from the introduction of machinery and new classes of workers. A few other organisations, such as the Bookbinders, are old, but are little more than friendly societies. A large number of small organisations have sprung up within the last three years.

"The wave of organisation among dock-labourers has been checked, on the Clyde, by the presence of a strong 'blackleg' society, partly due, no doubt, to the extravagant measures pursued by the local dockers' leaders. The miners, who in this neighbourhood are largely recruited from the ranks of un-skilled labour (frequently Irish), have not been

galvanised into unionism by the spasmodic efforts
of political agitators and 'men of straw'. There
appears to be no miners' union worth the name
throughout all the West of Scotland.

"The attempts of the larger trades at better
organisation are greatly hindered by the national
jealousy of any English headquarters, which often
prevents amalgamation, sometimes creates seces-
sions, and usually appears to check numerical growth.
This international jealousy is supplemented by a
scarcely concealed rivalry between Glasgow and
Edinburgh. The clannish spirit of the Scottish
worker militates against national organisation.

"One's general impression is that the Scottish
working men are still largely individualist in temperament, only thrashed temporarily into trade unionism
by severe depressions, or tempted into it by big
bribes. The best men, even if in the union, do not
devote themselves to its affairs, or otherwise to
raising their class, but seek to become small masters,
and very often succeed in rising to wealth. Hence
the paucity of able men in the ranks of union
officials. On the other hand, co-operation succeeds
in all respects, though there has been a striking
absence of attempts at the self-governing workshop. Cheap articles and high dividends are apparently much more potent in convincing the Scottish
workman of the benefits of association than any of
the promises of trade unionism."[1]

[1] This survey, with others, is among our Trade Union MSS. at the
London School of Economics.

And here are some general impressions on English Local Government; taken from diary entries of 1899:

"How much have I learnt in six weeks investigation?

"A vision of the tangle of Local Government: of the independence of the County Boroughs, the recalcitrant defiance of the Non-County Boroughs and the shadowy authority exercised over them by the County Councils; the grumblings of the District Councils at the C.C.'s proddings, the appeals of the Parish Councils to the C.C. against the neglect of work by the District Councils—the universal rivalry and sometimes actual litigation between various grades of sanitary authorities over incorporations and extensions of boundaries, over water catchment areas, tramways, and hospitals. Then again the mechanical grindings of the School Board and the short-sighted stinginess of the Boards of Guardians; and in the dim and distant Whitehall the old-womanish L.G.B., threatening, obstructing, auditing, and reporting—mostly without effect. It is not a vision of lucid beauty: but it is intensely human (MS. Diary, 16th May, 1899).

"Five weeks in Manchester in a little rented house, with our own maids to look after us and our secretary to help us—a peaceful happy time, collecting material and, by a well-regulated life, keeping fit for persistent work. We are more interested in this enquiry than in trade unionism: the problems are multitudinous and the machinery intricate. The least invigorating part of the subject-matter are the persons engaged in the work of local government:

in the present administration of English provincial local government there is a singular lack of idealism and charm, of efficiency and force.

"The Manchester Town Council turns out to be no better than that of Leeds. The most marked feature is the way in which the magnitude and importance of its work has outgrown its organisation. The different parts of the machine are out of joint; it rumbles on in some sort of fashion, because it is pushed along by outside pressure, but it is always breaking down in the efficiency of its administration. The council, judged by this fact, would seem to be inefficient or corrupt, or both. The men running the organisation are not a bad lot: one or two of the officials are distinctly able. But there is no head to the concern, no one who corresponds to a general manager of a railway company, still less to its paid chairman. The mayor, elected for one year, has all his time absorbed by public meetings, social functions, or routine administration: he is far more the ceremonial Head of the City than the chief of the executive of the city government. The town clerk and his deputy are exclusively engaged in legal and parliamentary business; they spend most of their time in the lobbies of the House of Commons, in presenting the Corporation's case at L.G.B. enquiries; in preparing leases and drafting agreements, or in submitting bye-laws to government departments. The suggestion that the town clerk of a great city like Manchester can be anything more than its solicitor and parliamentary agent—

can fill the place of its chief executive officer—is, as things are at present, an absurdity. All the other city officers are technicians—accountants, engineers, and medical men. The city surveyor and the medical officer of health are neither of them markedly competent, and they have the status, not of administrators but only of consultants—called in whenever the chairman or secretary of one of the standing committees deems their advice necessary. The city treasurer is a promoted clerk; the chief constable a promoted policeman. With one exception the administrative head of a department is the secretary of the committee supervising its work. Hence the services of gas and of water, of tramways and markets, and even the rivers department, are all managed by promoted clerks with no professional training for their work. In fact, there is only one real executive officer who understands the technique that he has to supervise—a man named Rook, the superintendent of the sanitary department, who, though he entered the council's service at 30s. a week, has become a technician at his own job, and may be trusted to see that any given piece of work is carried through from its inception to its completion. To make confusion worse confounded, each committee considers itself like an independent company, and reports as little as it dare to the Town Council, which meets once a month, and is regarded by the chairman and members of each committee as a superfluous body which ought not to intervene. These committees nominate their own

members for re-election each year, and the tradition
is that the committee must always be united in face
of the council. Hence the atmosphere of secretiveness towards the council and of suspicious hostility
on the part of those members of the council who do
not happen to be elected on to the leading committees. Some of the committees are dominated by
persons who are grotesquely unfit: for instance, the
Markets Committee has had for years an illiterate
tailor as chairman. In other cases the committee
is run by a really able and upright man, but even
he will pride himself on managing it 'as I should my
own business'; he resents mightily any criticism of
his policy or methods. In short, there is no body
whose special business it is to see that all parts of
the organisation are co-ordinated and working to
a common end. Friction and petty scandals, accusa-
tions and recriminations, dog the council's work.
And all this secretiveness and jealousy of control
does not attain its object—if that be a quiet administrative life. Tales of peculation and jobbery, most
of which are, I believe, untrue, get abroad through a
malicious member or a resentful elective auditor who
finds the accounts too much for his understanding.
The rejoinder of the committees to all these stories,
true or false, is always still more secrecy, with the
result that the council become enveloped in a permanent cloud of presumed stupidity and corruption.

"So far as we have made the acquaintance of the
councillors there are none very good and none very
bad: I have not picked out any who seem to be

'rotters'. The abler among them are all old men—a little gang of Liberals who are still the salt of the Council. The social status is predominantly lower middle class, a Tory solicitor and an I.L.P. journalist being the only men with any pretension to culture. The abler administrators have no pretension to ideas, hardly any to grammar: they are merely hardheaded shopkeepers, divided in their minds between their desire to keep the rates down and their ambition to magnify the importance of Manchester as against other cities. There is no cleavage on the council according to policy—the council drifts into subsidising the canal or working its own tramways, or into direct labour in its public works, almost without deliberate thought, and certainly without any discussion either of principles or of the special circumstances which make for or against the proposal before the council. The council, in fact, rumbles along by the method of trial and error: but it has its head in the right direction pushed by outside forces. But who is initiating this force? There seems no person or group of persons at work. It is more like the result of an impersonal current of ideas affecting all the persons concerned without their being conscious of them."[1]

We know not how the foregoing samples will appear to the studious reader. Some may dismiss these

[1] MS. Diary, 9th September 1899.

It must not be imagined that Manchester municipal government has not greatly improved since 1899. A more recent description will be found in *A City Council from Within*, by (Sir) E. D. Simon, 1926.

unconsidered and unchecked reports as mere journalism. Except for the fact that they were jotted down as rough memoranda for our own use, without any intention to publish, the epithet is warranted. The extracts from the American diary, for instance, do not differ, except by way of inferiority in scope and style, from the vivid descriptions of American municipal government contributed soon afterwards to contemporary magazines by Mr. Lincoln Steffens, and subsequently made up into a volume called *The Shame of the Cities*. This brilliant journalist had obviously better equipment in foreknowledge, and far greater and more varied opportunities for observation, than a couple of foreign tourists casually passing from New York to San Francisco. In our leisurely journey round the Anglo-Saxon world in 1898, it never occurred to us that we were engaged in scientific research. What we were doing was amusing ourselves by a "busman's holiday", during which we attended the sittings of about forty different representative assemblies. Anyone who objects that such hasty and unconsidered observations, without verification, ought not to be cited as evidence—perhaps not even published in the usual travel journal—has our full concurrence.

It would, however, be a mistake to dismiss, as useless to the investigator, first impressions of this sort. In our own case we have found them of considerable value. In the first place, they indicate points into which enquiry should be made, and which might not otherwise have been thought of. They draw attention to omissions. They suggest hypotheses to be tested on other examples. Although they possess in themselves no more evidential value than the scandalous allegations of a sensational newspaper, they may show us the track. When supplemented by the more trustworthy methods of investigation that we have described—the scrutiny of official records and other documents, the skilled interrogation of competent witnesses, and the use of statistics—personal observation of the institution at work may be transformed into unimpeachable truth. After all, it is, at worst, as good a basis to build on as the "contemporaneous literature" of books and journals, novels and poems, pamphlets and sermons, plays and newspapers, that we have described[1] as a valuable auxiliary to the official records. It is, at least, open to the investigator, on his holiday, to write some "contemporaneous literature" for his own use, and even for consultation by those who come after him.

But such first impressions, when gained on a foreign trip or by personal observation of any new field, have also another and an even more important utility. They make the investigator aware of the limits to be set to his generalisations. For centuries prior to Captain Cook, the European naturalists had described the swan as invariably having, among other attributes, that of whiteness. When travellers at last got to Australia they saw, for the first time, a swan that was black. Even our hasty impressions of American municipal institutions in 1898 came in

[1] See Chapter V.

useful during the succeeding years when we had to generalise on municipal institutions in England and Wales. What we have gained in our travels has not been any scientific knowledge of the institutions of other countries (and for this reason we have never published a book about them), but merely suggestions and hypotheses for the investigation of those amid which we live.

CHAPTER IX

THE USE OF STATISTICS

WE are not competent, either by mental equipment or by experience, to deal with what is sometimes termed the Statistical Method.[1] The special subjects to which our own work has been devoted, namely, the growth and development of such social institutions as the co-operative movement, trade unionism, and democratic government in Great Britain, whilst calling for the use of all available statistics, did not seem to us to afford much scope for statistical methods of investigation. We should be sorry to attempt to assess the relative value of the special work of the statistician and that of the sociologist employing other methods. It is clearly the duty of the sociological investigator to make all possible use of the statistics that the statistician supplies. But what

[1] We confine ourselves to the use of statistics already prepared, as we have no experience of the compilation and tabulation of new statistics. We advise the reader to consult the works of Professor A. L. Bowley (especially his *Elements of Statistics*, 5th edition, 1926; and *The Nature and Purpose of the Measurement of Social Phenomena*, 2nd edition, 1923). See also (especially for correlation) *Introduction to the Methods of Economic Statistics*, by W. L. Crum and A. C. Patton, 1925; and *Statistical Methods*, by Professors Truman and Kelley, New York, 1923.

does the statistician supply to sociology, and in what way can it be best used?

The method of the statistician, it has been said, is "the quantitative observation of aggregates".[1] Such statistical results as are afforded by the periodical census of the population, together with the totals, within a defined area, of registered births, marriages, and deaths, are valuable to the social student, not merely as helping in his perpetual duty of classification and verification, but also as suggesting hypotheses for further exploration. But statistics, in their use by the sociological investigator, call for special caution. Nothing is further from the truth than the notion that a table of figures affords, in itself, positive proof or disproof of any assertion or generalisation whatsoever. We may pass over the usual lack of certainty as to how the enumeration has been made, and what precautions have been taken to ensure accuracy alike in the collection of the facts and the computation of the totals. Assuming that the statistics have been honestly compiled and scientifically dealt with, there is still the limitation that the "aggregates" cover only those attributes common to all the units—those features in which the units are identical one with another. The evidence of fact that the statistics afford is accordingly limited to such identities. It is true that, by many subdivisions, homogeneity in a number of attributes can be obtained,

---

[1] See the paper by Dr. Mayr in *Journal of the Royal Statistical Society* for September 1883; also *Scope and Method of Political Economy*, by J. N. Keynes, 1891, p. 320.

as when the census gives "person, male, aged 35-45, Coventry, 1921, employed, motors and cycles". But the human beings counted in the census, or registered as being born, getting married, or ceasing to live, have, however, innumerable other attributes, in which they differ from each other; and it is often these widely differing attributes, or some among them, that form the basis of social classification. It is a common error to employ the statistical totals of aggregates as if they afforded information on the undivided and untabulated individual or class peculiarities. Thus the total number of births in Great Britain in two given years, or even the ratio of births to the population, can afford no proof that the birth-rate in the families of Jews or Catholics, or of professors or women graduates, is increasing or decreasing or stationary. But although throwing no light on the birth-rate of any particular section of the population of Great Britain, the figures for the whole nation or for particular localities may be fruitful of discovery in two ways. Even the statistics for a single year afford a basis of comparison with which, when particular sectional birth-rates are otherwise obtained, these may be usefully contrasted; and the comparison of those for a series of years may suggest new hypotheses to the investigator. It is for such uses, rather than with any idea of obtaining any conclusive proof of the validity of his generalisations, that the social investigator should make a point of collecting and displaying among his sheets of notes every shred of statistical information that he can obtain even remotely relating to the social institution with which his study is concerned.

Nor should the social investigator be discouraged from availing himself of statistics that fall much further short of perfection than the present British Census. All statistics concerned with social institutions suffer from the inherent defect that it is practically impossible to achieve an entirely water-tight definition of the class or classes of units which the statistician attempts to enumerate; and it is even difficult to ensure that the definition adopted is uniformly understood by all the enumerators and computers, and that it is not forgotten by those who reproduce the statistics, and not misunderstood by their readers. This defect, however, does not make the statistician's tables wholly valueless to the sociologist. "It is a well-known maxim of statistics", Professor Bowley tells us, "that we can study changes even when the definition or the enumeration is faulty."[1] Not only vital statistics of all sorts, but also statistics of membership of such organisations as co-operative societies and trade unions, and of their financial transactions, with all their manifold imperfections, will be useful, if repeated at intervals, as affording hypotheses relating to growth or development. For the sole purpose of comparison over a series of years uncertainties of definition and classification relating to the same social institutions, like simple errors of enumeration and computation—

[1] *The Measurement of Social Phenomena*, by A. L. Bowley, 1915, p. 151.

even the unintentional perversions due to unconscious bias—where these are so far recurrent as to
be, so to speak, chronic, may safely be ignored.

For such comparisons it is, however, supremely
important that there should have been constancy in
the definitions used. In the statistics of British Unemployment Insurance, for instance, the limits of
the class of "insured unemployed persons" have been
repeatedly changed in such a way as to vitiate comparison of one year with another. In fact, some
knowledge of the technique and history of the
figures, as well as of the exact meaning of the terms
used, is indispensable for any accurate quotation.

Another aspect of the relation of statistical work
to social investigation is well exemplified in Charles
Booth's "Grand Inquest" into the economic and
social condition of the whole population of London[1]
—probably the greatest statistical enterprise ever
attempted by a private person at his own expense.
Here the significant conception—one of very distinct
originality—was not that of simple enumeration of
every unit of a defined class, but the placing of the
results of elaborate personal observation of differing
units within a comprehensive statistical framework.
All sorts of enquirers into poverty—philanthropists,

---

[1] The outcome of this gigantic enterprise is recorded in *Life and Labour
of the People of London*, by Charles Booth, definitive edition in 17 volumes,
1902–3. An analytic description of the origin, methods, and results will be
found in *My Apprenticeship*, by Beatrice Webb, 1926, chap. v. pp. 216-56.

For another example, in a very different field, of the placing of
qualitative descriptions in a statistical framework, see *The Material
Culture and Social Conditions of the Simpler Peoples*, by L. T. Hobhouse,
G. C. Wheeler, and M. Ginsberg, 1930.

religious enthusiasts, charitable workers, medical practitioners, and socialist agitators—had from time to time given heart-rending accounts of suffering and want among the poor of great cities, and especially of London. But no one knew whether these sensational descriptions of particular cases were typical of any considerable proportion of the manual workers, or even how numerous they were; still less whether they were, as some said, a steadily growing host, or, on the contrary, merely the declining remnant of what had, in previous generations, been an actual majority of the whole wage-earning class.

In seeking an answer to these questions, Charles Booth turned first to the census and such other official statistics as were available, but found nothing in these "quantitative measurements of aggregates" that gave the information desired. He saw that what he needed was nothing less than the detailed particulars of the vocation, the income, the number of dependants, and the number of rooms occupied in the case of every working-class family. Only with these particulars could he make a sufficiently accurate classification of families according to social and economic position, which would reveal what number and what proportion were at or below a given "Poverty Line". To obtain this huge mass of information for the whole four millions of London's people by personal observation, even by the employment of an extensive group of assistants, was plainly impossible within a life-time. With great originality and extraordinary courage and persistence, Charles

Booth devised and carried out his investigation by what may be termed the Method of Wholesale Interviewing. As he modestly puts it: "The root idea with which I began the work was that every fact I needed was known to someone, and that the information had simply to be collected and put together".[1] As every family occupying premises rated at not more than £40 a year was known to the school attendance officers, then some 400 in number, Charles Booth obtained permission from the London School Board to arrange with them to give him, from their notebooks and their recollections, family by family, under endless personal interrogation by himself or one of his secretaries, all the particulars required. These particulars could then be checked and corrected by further "Wholesale Interviewing" of the police, the rate collectors, the sanitary inspectors, the school teachers, the investigators of the Charity Organisation Society, the hospital almoners, the officers of trade unions and friendly societies, the agents of the sewing-machine manufacturers, and, in fact, the officers of any organisation dealing extensively with the wage-earning class, together with individual personal observation of particular streets and even particular households when exceptionally required. The census could then be elucidated by a classification of its economically meaningless aggregates into eight social classes, their several totals and percentages showing with convincing accuracy

---

[1] *Life and Labour of the People in London*, new edition, 1903, final volume, p. 32; *My Apprenticeship*, by Beatrice Webb, 1926, p. 228.

how large was the number and proportion falling below the arbitrarily assumed "Poverty Line" of about 20s. per week family income. The sensational accounts of poverty, together with many other observations as to social condition, were thus, for the first time, given arithmetical precision.

But although Charles Booth, by setting a qualitative classification of the population into a statistical framework, gave each part of this qualitative description a definite arithmetical valuation, there was still no answer to the enquiry whether the quantity was greater or less than at any previous period, and whether in proportion to the total population it was increasing or decreasing. His statistical achievement, valuable though it was, had the shortcoming of presenting only a statical description of a changing mass of dynamic phenomena—a photograph of a single stage in what was a continuous growth.[1] It was in order to make good this shortcoming in Charles Booth's work that the London School of Economics undertook its "New Survey" of London, which, carried out in 1928–32 on lines similar to those followed in 1881–1902, is yielding an invaluable statistical comparison of the results at forty years interval, from which we can learn, not only what the position now is, but in what way it has been changing. The two surveys taken together

[1] "My principal aim is still confined to the description of things as they are. I have not undertaken to investigate how they came to be so, nor, except incidentally, to indicate whither they are tending, and only to a very limited extent, or very occasionally, has any comparison been made with the past." (*Life and Labour of the People of London*, by Charles Booth; *My Apprenticeship*, by Beatrice Webb, 1926, p. 245.)

afford, on point after point, a whole series of new hypotheses as to the causes and effects of such social developments.[1]

A further improvement that Charles Booth might have made, and thereby effected a great economy in time and effort, is the substitution of sampling for complete enumeration.[2] When nothing more is required than classification, with approximate percentages of the total population, it has been abundantly demonstrated that an adequate series of samples, taken quite mechanically so as to avoid all influence of unconscious bias, gives results of perfect accuracy within the prescribed limits. What is vitally important in sampling is that the population or other aggregate to be dealt with should be rigidly defined, and that every unit should have an equal chance of being included in the sample. When Professor Bowley wished to discover what was the social condition of the population of five separate towns of England, he found that an investigation of 5 per cent of all the households, choosing the twentieth, fortieth, sixtieth, and so on from the complete list, gave him, for the special purposes of his investigation, a sufficiently accurate picture of the

---

[1] Two volumes have already been published under the title of *The New Survey of London Life and Labour*, vols. i. and ii. 1930–1, edited by Sir Hubert Llewellyn Smith, K.C.B.

[2] For a further description of the Method of Sampling, and of the conditions upon which it can usefully be adopted, the student should consult *The Elements of Statistics*, 5th edition, 1928, and *The Nature and Purpose of Measurement of Social Phenomena*, 2nd edition, 1923, both by A. L. Bowley; *Livelihood and Poverty*, by A. L. Bowley and A. R. Burnett-Hurst, 1915; and *Has Poverty Diminished?* by A. L. Bowley and M. H. Hogg, 1925.

whole, with the provision that there was a lack of precision the importance of which could be estimated. In such a case the percentage could be known in round numbers (28 per cent), but not so precisely as to a thousandth part (*e.g.* 28·3 per cent). With larger numbers and wider dispersion by localities and vocations, even a smaller sample than 5 per cent suffices. When the Ministry of Labour wished in 1924, 1927, and 1931 to discover what was the frequency and the duration of the spells of unemployment of the ten or twelve millions of men and women on the insurance registers, or of the one to three millions among them who were at a given time unemployed, together with the ages and estimated efficiency of each section, it was found practicable to take as samples the cases entered on the first page of each of several hundred volumes of records in which the particulars of all the millions were consecutively entered. In this way an absolutely unbiassed series of samples, comprising in the earlier years 1 per cent of the aggregate, and in the third enquiry (that concerning nearly two and three-quarter millions in 1931) only ½ per cent, was found to give a sufficiently accurate picture of the whole mass for all the purposes for which it was required.[1]

The Method of Sampling can, of course, be adopted for other than numerical enquiries. We have mentioned elsewhere our own employment of this device

[1] See the Report (summarised in *Labour Gazette*, January 1932) published in the volume entitled *Appendices to the Minutes of Evidence taken before the Royal Commission on Unemployment Insurance*, Part V. (Stationery Office, 1932).

in our investigation of the provisions contained in the thousands of local Acts which transformed a large part of the municipal administration of the English towns (and also that of the poor law in half a hundred localities) between 1689 and 1834. We had a complete analysis made of all these Acts during selected years, taking a particular year in each decade throughout the whole period. This analysis, when displayed on a series of separate sheets of paper, not only revealed at a glance the decade in which particular provisions began to be inserted in these Acts—a discovery which could then be verified and rendered precise by detailed inspection, on this point only, of the Acts of previous years—but also suggested new hypotheses for further exploration, and for comparison with other evidence, as to the local circumstances in which each set of provisions had been found desirable in the various localities.

Although the social investigator finds himself dealing with many details concerning social institutions in their growth and development, which are not susceptible to quantitative statistics—that is to say with attributes which are exclusively qualitative— he is not without the means of accurately placing them in comparison with other entities having attributes of like nature. As Professor Bowley reminds us: "The possibilities of description are not exhausted even when no unit (of measurement) can be devised, for objects can be placed in order without any measured scale." He gives as an example the teacher's customary classification of his pupils according to his own vague and general impression of their intellectual powers. Such a competent teacher, Professor Bowley says, "could place a class in order of intelligence with as much certainty as any system of examination marks would afford". In a similar way, in the course of our own studies, we have frequently placed, tentatively, in order among themselves, various Trade Unions, Co-operative Societies, English municipalities, Poor Law Unions, and what not, according to our impression of their possession of particular qualities, which were not measurable by statistics. Such a tentative placing in order of a number of entities for which no statistical data can be assigned may be helpful in suggesting hypothetical comparisons which it may be found possible to verify or disprove by other forms of evidence. And the placing in order may be exceedingly precise. "If we have", Professor Bowley observes, "thus placed persons or things in order, we may proceed in either of two ways. We may assign classes, describe their characteristics, and then allot an individual to a class, named either by adjective (*e.g.* poor), or artificially (as 4th or D class). Or we may use Galton's method of percentiles, and having selected persons, say one-hundredth, one-quarter or one-half up the scale, describe these persons by whatever method is practicable."[1]

It is, in fact, a common error to suppose that whenever it is impracticable to obtain complete statistics,

---

[1] *The Measurement of Social Phenomena*, by A. L. Bowley, 1915, pp. 10-11.

or statistics which can only be relied on as accurate over a part of the field, no use whatever can be made of them. If this were the case, no statistics dealing with large numbers could ever be employed. Even the British Census, after 130 years of experience, and many successive improvements, necessarily enshrines innumerable inaccuracies of enumeration, of definition, and of classification. But for practical purposes the inaccuracies are of such a nature that they do not matter.

We have, for instance, already mentioned the use of statistics relating to the same subject-matter at two or more different dates. We can often study changes by the use of statistics even when the definition or the enumeration is known to be defective. It is, however, usually so difficult to be sure that there has been no change in the definition, and no alteration in the measures of capacity, weight, or price between the dates chosen for comparison, that the statistical differences of this kind can properly be taken only as hypotheses to be tested by other available evidence.

Moreover, if the investigator can satisfy himself as to the kind and degree of inaccuracy from which the statistics suffer, he may take care to employ them as evidence or in argument, only in the manner and to the extent in which the probable inaccuracies are irrelevant. Professor Bowley gives an illustration of "the strictest method" of thus employing imperfect statistics, which he says "might be called the use of the margin of uncertainties. Suppose that the definition has been carefully drawn, and we turn to available statistics, we may find that 10,000,000 people certainly satisfy the definition, that another 100,000 probably satisfy it, and that there may be not more than 50,000 in addition who may satisfy it for all we know. We should then be able to say that between 10,000,000 less 1 per cent and 10,100,000 less $\frac{1}{2}$ per cent satisfied the definition; and we could keep this margin throughout any calculation, till we could tell whether it was of any ultimate importance".[1]

Such imperfect statistics, with their "marginal uncertainties" brought forcibly to the mind of the investigator, may actually be fruitful in suggesting hypotheses in connection either with the unenumerated residues or with the enumerated aggregates themselves.

There remains a final observation on the statistical contribution to social investigation, which every investigator, be he expert statistician or unmathematical sociologist, ought always to bear in mind. The results of any statistical process, however scientifically it is devised and performed, will depend essentially on the data subjected to it. If the data are false, either by inaccuracy or insufficiency, the results of the statistical manipulation of them cannot possibly be true. The quality of what is ground out by the most perfect sausage-machine depends on the material supplied to it. Moreover, the validity of the "quantitative observation of aggregates", with which the statistician is concerned, depends

[1] *The Measurement of Social Phenomena*, by A. L. Bowley, 1915, p. 20.

essentially upon the qualitative as well as the quantitative identity of the units making up the aggregates. But in real life the units never are in all respects qualitatively identical. The dangerous disease to which all statistics are liable, and from which few entirely escape, is the tacit assumption that the units are more completely identical than in fact they are, leading to the consequent extension of statistical results to a wider predication than can accurately be obtained out of the data. Hence the character and relevance, the accuracy and sufficiency of the data which the statistician takes for the material of his processes (or which his sociological colleague may supply to him in order that he may "work out the sums") ought to be the subject of most serious examination and consideration before the statistical process is begun. It is to be feared that this is too frequently neglected. No statistical method will enable the collection of facts to be dispensed with, nor their qualitative analysis to be slurred over, nor the processes of provisional classification and the formation of tentative hypotheses to be neglected, nor the various alternative methods of verification to be ignored. If what is aimed at is not merely the purification or refinement of existing knowledge, but actually the discovery of new truth hitherto unsuspected by the world, no arithmetical or mathematical analysis or manipulation of what is already known will, by itself, win something from the unknown. Mathematics, once observed to the authors no less a statistician than the late Professor

F. Y. Edgeworth, may reveal error; it can never, of itself, discover unsuspected new truth. The most that can be got out of a mathematical calculation in the way of discovery is, notably on the revelation of some unanticipated residue, a hint towards a new hypothesis, which can then be tested by observation and experiment.

CHAPTER X

To the investigator in the physical sciences or in biology it would be unnecessary to insist on the supreme importance, in the scientific method, of the stage of verification. Nothing can be accounted a discovery—usually nothing should be published to the world about what seems to be a discovery—until it has been deliberately and exhaustively tested, to the utmost of the investigator's ability, by systematic comparison with the facts, as revealed either in crucial experiments when these are possible, or else by independent testimony or systematic further enquiries. Social students have unfortunately had, in the past, much less regard to verification than their colleagues in other sciences; largely owing, it must be said, to the exceptional difficulties of the process.

In the learned treatises on logic, as in Professor Graham Wallas's instructive *Art of Thought*, the authors' references to verification appear principally and, indeed, usually to have in view what they seem to regard as the final stage in the method of discovery, namely, that of transforming a hypothetical generalisation into a demonstrated theory, or even a "law of nature". The more modest sociological investigator does not find himself talking about laws of nature, and he is cautious even about making sweeping generalisations. He realises that his particular science is, at present, far from the stage reached by physics or chemistry; and that it stands, perhaps, about where "natural history" did in the age of Cuvier or that of Buffon.[1]

In our own experience we have found that verification is, in one or other form, essential, not merely at one stage, but actually at all stages of social investigation. The inability of the sociologist to apply any yardstick to a social institution, or even to measure, with mathematical accuracy, the facts about it that he obtains, makes it impossible to place reliance on any single observation, whether of his own or by other people. The limited use that can be made of experiment, as we shall presently describe, renders indispensable a constant habit of comparing one qualitative observation with another. This accumulation of many observations, though possibly merely qualitative, or capable of only im-

---

[1] "Two hundred years ago the physicists and chemists were beginning to study the properties of metals by exact methods involving measurement, and the biologists were looking down the first microscopes. But the real knowledge of metals lay in the hands of skilled workmen, who handed down their rule-of-thumb methods and manual dexterity to their children. To-day metallurgy is a branch of applied science, while biologists are just beginning to be of some use to the practical animal breeder, though they cannot beat him at his own game. *Psychology is about as much more complex than biology as biology than physics.*" (*Possible Worlds*, by J. B. S. Haldane, 1927, p. 184.) We should say "still more sociology".

perfect measurement, may amount to quite effective verification; verification, it is true, of what the logician might deem a low order of probability, such as that on which most of the world's action proceeds. This demonstration of probability is, it must be confessed, often the only kind of verification that the sociologist can at present obtain.

THE USE OF EXPERIMENT

The social student is keenly conscious of his inability to employ, in the testing of his hypotheses, the method of experiment, in the sense in which that term is used by the investigator in the physical sciences, and, in our own day, in certain cases, also by the biologist and the psychologist. In sociological investigation there is practically never any possibility of a deliberately staged and scientifically controlled crucial experiment which can be repeated at will by the same experimenter or by other persons, not only in the same laboratory or observatory, but also in others throughout the civilised world. This is not to say that there is, in sociological investigation, nothing in the nature of verification by actual trial, which may be even continuous over a long term, and frequently repeated under differing conditions. Thus, there is actually a great deal of experiment, though of a different kind than that of the laboratory or observatory.[1] What the sociologist has principally to

---

[1] The sociologist cannot, as the biologist does, place his specimens on the dissecting table and experiment on them with his scalpel. On the other

experiment on is not matter or physical forces, but human behaviour, especially as manifested in social institutions which can be closely observed although not mathematically measured. Experiments of this sort are being made in every direction every day. The conduct of profit-making business on any but the smallest scale, whether in mining or growing, manufacture or trading, is one continual series of experiments, not only on nature, but especially on human nature, the results of which are closely watched, and often statistically measured, usually without any parade of science, but with a constant view to future modifications of practice. In modern capitalist enterprise on a large scale, this continuous scrutiny of the results upon human behaviour of what is often thought of as a process of "Trial and Error" takes form in highly systematised recording and elaborate statistical manipulation, not merely of output and sales, stocks and goods in transit, price, and profit, but also of the equally fluctuating use or consumption, per day or per unit of product, of materials, component parts, power, and human labour. Emerging from the device of an audit of cash, through the more complicated audit of stamps, stores, materials, and components, there is now a brand new art—that of costing—applied not only to products, but also to particular ingredients and components, and even to

hand, the biologist cannot, as the sociologist does, interrogate his specimens, analyse their replies, and check the facts thus elicited, not only by other responses but also by the written documents that the specimen itself, and others of like nature, have been secreting for their own purposes.

the need for repairs and renewals—the whole used as the basis of precise comparison between different processes, different types of machines and products, different departments or factories, and different places of production. On these statistical tables, diagrams, and curves, decisions are taken, and orders given day by day, each of which, whether or not it proves to increase profit, amounts to a real experiment in administration that will afford evidence confirming or contradicting the hypothesis that led to its execution. In other fields of business endeavour, no great advertiser proceeds otherwise than by a series of deliberate experiments on human behaviour, which are tried, successively, on different centres of population, with different commodities, through different channels of publicity, by different devices or in different forms of literary or pictorial expression, the results being often made the subject of ingeniously devised automatic record, continuously translated into instructive statistics. The whole mystery of currency and credit, through which the twentieth century world is painfully stumbling, depends on a series of assumptions as to the behaviour of men, based on past and contemporary experience, on which all the scientific psychology that we possess throws very little useful light. It is all the more confusing that such experiments have now to be made in societies living by international as well as national division of labour and exchange of products and services, through the medium of competitive salesmanship at competitive prices, adjusted by an imperfectly unified banking system carried on avowedly for the bankers' own profit. Yet their consequences cannot be ignored by any serious student. Every finance minister in every country tries a sociological experiment on the "curve of demand" and the people's several "scales of values" every time he imposes a new tax or remits an old one, or makes any change in its amount or its conditions. The laws and administrative departments regulating the employment of labour or the supply of pure water, unadulterated food, and authentic drugs, like those providing the social services so characteristic of every civilised country during the past hundred years, represent a whole series of experiments inspired by desire to bring about certain improvements in social organisation. All these experiments are based on deliberately formulated hypotheses as to the human nature of employers and wage-earners, doctors and patients, savers and spenders, and the working of particular social institutions. These hypotheses, when put into statutory form by hesitating legislators and doubting administrators, are successively verified or disproved, and the social institutions are, in fact, modified or simply extended, according to the ascertained results of these imperfectly observed, and even more imperfectly recorded, experiments on human behaviour.

We may, indeed, say that, far from there being, in sociology, no resort to experiment, there is, in fact, far more experimenting, and experimenting on a vastly greater scale, continuously carried on in the world sociological laboratory in which we all live, than by the numerous but relatively small physical, chemical, and biological laboratories that have been established within it. We emphasise again that this is not the carefully staged and scientifically controlled experiment of the physicist or chemist. Such social experiments as we have mentioned are, indeed, only part of the material—an invaluable part—of the sociologist, which he has to accept for observation with all their imperfections and irrelevant and confusing accompaniments. How can any social student even begin to consider the particular social institutions established in connection with the consumption of intoxicants without taking careful note of the experiments along the line of partial or complete prohibition, tried not only in the various Baltic States, but also, on a gigantic scale, with unexpected results, in the United States of America? Who can correctly appraise even the magnitude, range, and variety—let alone the effects and the value—of the series of ever-changing social experiments that the government of the Union of Socialist Soviet Republics has been conducting since 1917, in the pertinacious remodelling, from top to bottom, of all the political, the economic, the sexual, the cultural, and the ethical institutions of one-twelfth of the world's population, occupying one-sixth of its land surface?

These experiments on human behaviour, especially as manifested in the working of social institutions, are, of course, none the less, experiments,

because they are not put in operation by the sociological investigators themselves, but by persons in
authority as entrepreneurs, legislators, or ministers,
often having no consciousness of the experimental
nature of their work and no scientific interest in its
results.[1] But the way in which these sociological
experiments are, in fact, conducted greatly affects
their evidential value. Practically in no case are
they made by persons with any training in investigation or with due appreciation of their scientific
value as experiments. In no case are they exactly
the experiments that the scientific investigator
would have chosen to test his own hypotheses.
Those made in the course of capitalist business
enterprise are nearly always wrapped in secrecy and
accordingly yield nothing to science. Those carried
out by public authorities are seldom described with
precision, and the publication of their outcome is
in many ways imperfect.[2] In the results, as far as

---

[1] It is worth notice that all the social institutions resulting from experiments put in operation by directors of industry, legislators, and departmental ministers fall within the fourth class, which we have termed
the scientific or technical (see Chapter I.). Such institutions modify or
otherwise affect those arising from animal instinct, religious emotion, or
humanistic theory (our three other classes); but it seems that any new
institutions, so far created during the past hundred years, have essentially
the nature of the fourth class.

[2] One frequent imperfection in such social experiments is that the reports upon their results are made by the persons who, as ministers or civil
servants, managing directors or foremen, are themselves responsible for
the administration of the enterprise. With regard to the audit we have
long since learned that, to be trustworthy, it must always be conducted
by a professionally trained expert entirely unconnected with the administration. It is equally necessary that every experiment in administration,
and therefore the administration as a whole, should be made the subject
of continuous scrutiny and periodical detailed reports by independent
experts in no way responsible for the direction of policy or for current

made known, no allowance is or can be made, with any pretence at accuracy, for plurality of causes and intermixture of effects. No inference can be drawn with any certainty as to what would have happened under other conditions, in other places, at other times, or among people of other races, other religions, or other traditions. Finally, it must not be forgotten that peoples and circumstances are always changing, even whilst the experiments are actually in progress.

What the vast array of unscientific, and, so to speak, unintentional experiments in social administration yield to the student is not the certain verification that the physicist or the chemist may hope to obtain by his laboratory experiment, but something else. The capitalist, the legislator, or the departmental minister—who are, anyhow, perpetually taking action that alters social relations— are providing the sociological investigator with a continuous supply of invaluable material. The ploughman does not turn over the earth in order that the birds may pick up worms; but the birds none the less follow the plough. The student who

management. It is becoming more and more the practice in great business enterprises in the United States and Great Britain to have a highly organised statistical department, entirely unconnected with policy or its administration, and charged, not only with continuously auditing all the accounts and perpetually "costing" every factor in the enterprise, but also with periodically reporting on the results of particular experiments. The Government of the Union of Socialist Soviet Republics, which had merged its Central Statistical Bureau with its State Planning Board, has (1932) just established a new "Central Board of Accounting" to be independent of the State Planning Board and to report continuously to the highest governmental authorities, as to the actual results of the innumerable economic experiments in progress.

diligently follows the administrator's plough picks up new information of what the world is like; fresh ideas as to how social relations work; additional hypotheses about co-existences and sequences; and, last but not least, even suggestions towards partial confirmation or modification of some of the classifications or hypotheses upon which he has been tentatively proceeding. This may not amount to verification, in the sense that the physicist or chemist uses the term when, at last, he has the joy of conducting his own deliberately staged and scientifically controlled laboratory experiment in a genuinely crucial instance, which shall for ever irrefutably prove or disprove a confident hypothesis.[1] But although not providing verification in this sense, these unintentional public experiments, when combined with the other methods that we have described, none the less afford to sociology an effective and a potent instrument for discovery, of which it is indispensable that the investigator should make the fullest possible use.

[1] It may be observed that the experiments of the physicists, chemists, and biologists do not always yield the ideal certainty of verification. Bathybius and Koch's tubercle bacillus, though authentically discovered, could eventually not be traced. Thousands of analyses of atmospheric air had been used in the lecture room to demonstrate to hundreds of thousands of chemical students that it was entirely made up of oxygen and nitrogen, until Rayleigh and Ramsay, remembering Cavendish's earlier ascertainment of an inexplicable residue, by more precise measurement discovered that it contained also argon, and presently also other new gases. Even the astronomers' predictions of eclipses are, we believe, found, in the observatory, to be inaccurate. The eclipse always begins earlier or later than was expected! The error, it is true, is always a little one. But if even astronomical predictions prove faulty, though only to an insignificant extent, how can the predictions of the sociologist be expected to be quite accurate?

THE AGGREGATION OF EVIDENCE

The method by which the sociologist obtains all the verification that is open to him—at any rate in the present stage of his science—is a perpetual aggregation and comparison of evidence of different kinds and from different sources. For instance, we have described to what an extent the sociologist has to depend for his facts on the spoken word. Yet he has to realise from the outset that the spoken word is—or at least must be assumed to be—invariably inaccurate, or at best of quite uncertain evidential value. The employer, or even the foreman, who honestly informs the interviewer that the average wage of the persons employed in that establishment is fifteen dollars or fifty shillings per week is not aware that "of itself" an arithmetical average is more likely to conceal than to disclose important facts.[1] He naturally does not distinguish between boys or girls, unskilled labourers whether men or women; improvers or skilled craftsmen; superannuated workmen lingering on as messengers or gate-keepers; he makes no allowance for "lost time" or unemployment, holidays or illness, and equally none for overtime and other extras; and, finally, he does not in the least realise what precisely an average is or how it is obtained, and he is blissfully ignorant alike of the "mode" and the "median". Such information as to wages or earnings, to be gratefully accepted whenever proffered, but

[1] *The Measurement of Social Phenomena*, by A. L. Bowley, 1915, p. 46.

to be noted as a mere hypothesis, is, of course, useless
without minute analysis of the kinds of wage-
earners included, or without statistical verification
by the scrutiny of wages sheets, and by equally
rigorous comparison with the facts of other establishments, at the same and at other dates, in the
same and in other places, and belonging to the same
and to other industries. Or, to take the investigation in a different field, how much reliance can the
foreign enquirer—even so well informed and expert
a one as President Lawrence Lowell or Professor
Élie Halévy—place upon oral statements made to
him as to what is the British constitution, whether
they are enunciated by British politicians, academic
philosophers, discreet civil servants, or ministers of
the Crown? The British investigator can get, in
response to his enquiries, no more completely
accurate oral information on such a subject than
does the foreigner. But the native is better able than
the foreigner to check and amplify these statements
by his own general knowledge. He listens to them
much more in order to gain hints as to the points
to be further investigated than as facts to be
garnered and enshrined in a book. In fact, they become the basis of new tentative hypotheses which
he seeks to verify by further investigation. He tests
them by the documents, by official statistics, by the
legal text-books, by the descriptions afforded by
contemporaneous literature, and finally by collation
of the oral statements by other informants made
in response to his more precise enquiries on the

minute "residues" of uncertainty still left in his discriminating mind. The written word (but only in the document as we have defined it, not in contemporaneous literature) is usually of higher evidential value than the spoken word. But it is equally in need of verification. It may, indeed, supply authentic evidence of isolated facts, but facts, like jewels, depend on their setting. Lord Acton remarked that "Facts are intelligible and instructive . . . *when they are seen not merely as they follow, but as they correspond; not merely as they have happened, but as they are paralleled*".[1] Thus, what the experienced investigator derives from the document is, in the first place, only a provisional hypothesis to be subsequently verified. What is the meaning of the dry and, doubtless, accurate official record, made without intention to deceive, or even to inform the historical researcher? Can he be sure that he understands exactly what was the nature of the facts that the record purports to describe? Did the terms used by the scribe—even the measurements given in the record—have the import that they convey to the reader of another century, another country, or another race? Here, too, the experienced student notes also, but merely as one more hypothesis, the way in which he himself at first sight interprets the record, for verification by comparison with other entries in the same record, by explanatory entries in other records, in the light of the relevant references to be found in con-

[1] *The History of Freedom and Other Essays*, by Lord Acton, 1907, p. 254.

temporaneous literature of the same or of different dates, in the same or in another country.[1]

At the same time it has to be borne in mind, in the process of verification, that in the whole province of sociology no hypothesis, whether in the form of classification or of prediction, can ever be expected to prove true or valid up to the extreme limit of its possible application. It may be inconceivable to the mathematician, and incomprehensible to the logician, but it is characteristic of every proposition in sociology—whether hypothesis or classification, whether generalisation or "natural law", whether principle or copy-book maxim, whether popular proverb or nursery rhyme—that it is subject (as the economists declared the cultivation of land to be) to the "Law of Diminishing Returns". Pursued too far in application, or pressed too hard, eventually it reaches the "Margin of Cultivation", where it fails any longer to correspond with the facts; at which point, indeed, some other generalisation or principle becomes of greater validity or force.

It will be seen that the verification to be made by the sociological investigator differs essentially in form from the kind of verification expected of the student in the physical sciences. But verification in sociology demands, we think, both a larger proportion of the time of the investigator, and a more

[1] "In order to understand a document we must know the language of the time, that is, the meanings of words and forms of expression in use at the time when the text was written. *The meaning of a word is to be determined by bringing together the passages where it is employed.*" (*Introduction to the Study of History*, by C. Langlois and C. Seignobos, translated by G. G. Berry, 1898, p. 147.)

incessant use of his attention, than is the case in physics, chemistry, or biology. Although the sociologist can seldom, if ever, make his own experiments, he has many more of the experiments of other people—those always being made in business or public administration—to scrutinise than his colleague in the simpler sciences. The experiments in the sociological sphere which have to be watched are much more difficult to interpret than those of the laboratory. Moreover, the sociologist has to use the powers of verification that are open to him, including this perpetual scrutiny of the unintentional experiments that are always being conducted, not only at that supreme moment of his enquiries, but much more than the physicist, the chemist, or the biologist, at all stages of investigation; not merely as to the validity of his discoveries, but actually also as to the accuracy of the facts that he laboriously extracts, not merely to free himself from the mistakes due to his own personal equation, but even more seriously to avoid accepting as facts what are not facts, and importing into them meanings that they do not bear.

To sum up, verification, to the social investigator, is indispensable at all stages of his work, primarily to fortify every one of his assertions. He must verify all his facts, even those that he has himself observed. He must verify, by independent testimony, every judgment made by the practical man in his own business,[1] and every other statement put forward

---

[1] "Never has the judgment of the practitioner as such any immediate scientific value: it must invariably be taken only as a subject for investi-

as evidence. He must verify every one of his hypothetical classifications before he can confidently put
forward even a statical description of any part of
the social institution that he is studying. Still more
necessary is verification before he ventures on
dynamic descriptions, involving hypotheses as to
sequences. Few and far between, or at least very
tentative and general, are the generalisations
which the sociologist is yet warranted in dogmatically making as to causation. His discoveries, at
least in the present stage of his science, and with all
the verification that is open to him, must be limited
to tendencies, producing results as to which he can,
with any confidence, predicate only a low order of
probability. Yet in all these respects, the sociologist
is no worse off than the biologist was less than a century ago!

gation." (*Wie studirt man Sozialwissenschaft*, by Josef Schumpeter, 1915,
p. 43.)

CHAPTER XI

IT is unusual to include, in a description of scientific method, the final stage of publication. Our purpose in emphasising this stage, as actually the completion of the process, is partly to show how necessary is publication to ensure convincing verification, and partly to explain the special requirements in publication that are imposed on the sociological discoverer.

Until publication to the world, or at least to the scientific world, has been made, it can hardly be said that, in the widening of the bounds of knowledge, achievement has taken place. We cannot even speculate as to how much the world has lost through non-publication, whether because of fear of persecution or morbid secrecy, or merely procrastination and premature death. Roger Bacon is not the only discoverer who is believed to have had greater things to tell than any actually revealed. Only by the accidental preservation of their private records, and the publication of these in the nineteenth century, do we know of valuable biological observations actually made by such different geniuses as Leonardo da Vinci and Sir Thomas Browne, whose failure to publish what they alone could appreciate deprived the scientific world of light for three whole centuries. One of Newton's most notable achievements was his examination of the perturbations of the moon's orbit. For the progression of the apses Newton's calculation gave only one and a half degrees or half the observed amount. D'Alembert, Clairault, and others of the great analytical mathematicians attempted to account for this curious discrepancy, but arrived at the same result, till at last Clairault found that a number of terms had been omitted in the series as unimportant, which turned out to be not negligible, and when they were included the result was correct. It was not till Professor Adams, one of the discoverers of Neptune, was editing the Newton papers in the possession of the Earl of Portsmouth that MSS. were discovered showing that Newton had himself reworked the calculations and found out the cause of the error, *but had not published the correction.*[1]

But the great majority of manuscript notes, even of men of science, are destroyed at the death of their authors, and there are other causes of loss. We are told that William Harvey's notes on the generation of insects, which are believed to have contained discoveries not made again for a century or two,

[1] *Mechanics,* by J. Cox, 1904, pp. 95-6.

were wholly destroyed in a raid on his house during the Civil War.

A special reason for the publication, at least to the scientific world, of every new truth that the scientist thinks that he has found, and believes that he has verified, is that such publication is the only way in which complete verification can be unmistakably and unchallengeably effected. It is at once the boast and the glory of the modern scientific world that every discovery in astronomy, mechanics, physics, and chemistry, made in any country whatsoever, and published in the scientific journals of Western Europe or the United States,[1] is promptly put to the test of experiment or other appropriate searching trial by numbers of separate enquirers in every university and scientific laboratory throughout the world, any failure of verification being immediately reported and discussed in the scientific press. In the wide range of biology, from bacteriology right up to psychology—so far as these studies have become genuinely scientific—a like

---

[1] Scarcely more useful to the world than non-publication is publication in the obscurity of a language unread by other scientists (for this reason, Russian, Hungarian, Finnish, and Japanese scientists usually contribute papers to German, French, or English scientific journals); or only in small local journals, where Mendel's fundamental discoveries in genetics were buried for half a century; or (as has happened to scientists in government employment) only in official reports, not brought to the notice of fellow-workers in the subject. There is even a greater tragedy, namely, that of scientific discoveries described in papers submitted to contemporary masters on the subject, or even learned societies; but suppressed because the discoveries were deemed incredible. It is said that Waterston, in 1848, enunciated the kinetic theory of gases in a paper which the Royal Society failed to publish, so that nearly thirty years elapsed before the work was done over again by Clausius and Clerk Maxwell.

process of searching and testing verification of all published discoveries is now becoming habitual. It is not for sociologists to remain behind. It is just because social science stands so greatly in need of systematic and impersonal verification of every assumed extension, within its own sphere, of the bounds of knowledge—just because the very nature of the subject-matter makes it difficult for the individual thinker and discoverer to verify, without bias, his own conclusions in a manner convincing to those who have different personal equations or who have not participated in his work—that prompt publication of every such advance is of special obligation. Only by this means, it may be suggested, can sociology, as a science, ever attain the assured position enjoyed by its elder sisters.

Publication of sociological advances should, in order to obtain the result of widespread verification, take the form of precise and particular description of the novelty itself, with no more encircling verbosity than sufficient explanation to enable the place of the novelty in relation to the body of established knowledge to be immediately understood. Too often, during the past formative century of social science, both its greatest thinkers on the one hand and its most youthful enthusiasts on the other have embodied the outcome of their work in complete revisions, according to their individual standpoints, of the entire *corpus* of sociology as contemporaneously understood. This was made the subject of special reproach to sociology by Henry

Sidgwick in 1885,[1] who took as examples the elaborate treatises of Auguste Comte, Herbert Spencer, and Albert Schaeffle, each of whom had a different view of the scope and substance of the science as a whole. Whether the publication of these comprehensive treatises was, because of their very comprehensiveness, the most effective way to build up a commonly accepted body of sociological knowledge may be open to doubt. What they certainly did not secure, or even make practicable, was that widespread searching and testing, in all the universities of the world, of the validity of the particular new contributions to sociological science that their authors might have claimed to have made. The necessary universal verification, detached from all personal predilection, was not, in fact, obtained ; as we think, largely because publication did not take the most effective form.

The right form of publication is, in sociology, all the more necessary, just because perfect verification is specially hard to obtain. There does not exist, at present, even including every civilised country, anything like the crowd of eager investigators that, in chemistry or physics, stand ready and eager to test every new discovery. Moreover, the operation is, in sociology, specially difficult. Each particular novelty is not, like Rayleigh and Ramsay's discovery of argon, or Madam Curie's discovery of radio-activity, a laboratory achievement, which any

[1] *The Scope and Method of Economic Science*, by Henry Sidgwick, 1885, pp. 46-54.

competent scientist, merely by using the requisite care, can, in any adequately equipped laboratory, repeat over and over again for himself. And there is a further obstacle. We fear it must be admitted that many sociological investigators have not yet developed that willingness to accept with an open mind, still less to consider sympathetically, the hypotheses and the formulated theories of other sociologists, notably those of foreign countries, with a view to promptly putting them to the test of independent and disinterested verification. It is part of the same individualistic insularity which marks the work of many sociologists that the nascent science is still inadequately equipped with scientific journals able and willing to place before the scientific world all the minor additions to our knowledge, the accurate descriptions of new species and varieties, the continual revisions of classification, the suggestions of novel hypotheses, and other points for widespread investigation—all of which are valuable adjuncts to the process of discovery, even when themselves undeserving of the name.

The ideal form of publication would perhaps be a precise statement of the new conclusions as to the exact form or working of some definite example or manifestation of a particular social institution ; candidly inviting its verification or disproof at the hands of other investigators; giving the most minutely accurate description of structure and function, development and effects; and showing how these conclusions differ from those come to, on the same subject, by others who have written on it, whose published references thereto should all be enumerated.[1]

[1] Publication in this form would be facilitated if sociology had a widely circulated "International Abstract" journal, similar to those published for physics, chemistry, physiology, etc.

CHAPTER XII

THE RELATION OF SCIENCE TO THE PURPOSE
OF LIFE

Our description of the province of sociology, and
our account of the method by which, according
to our own experience, that province can best be
explored, may lead to further questions. Is the
scientific study of social organisation of any use to
the world? For the sociologist cannot ignore the fact
that many people who admit the practical utility
of physical science, which has given them, within
the present generation, useful new substances like
aluminium, and such delights as electric light and
"wireless", are sceptical about the value of sociology.
This new-fangled study, they say, may satisfy intellectual curiosity, but does not seem able to predict
even the result of a general election, let alone that
of a customs tariff or a prohibitory law. The sociologist, they declare, may, by what he calls his science,
accumulate a mass of knowledge, but can it be made
useful? Is an applied science of society possible?

We believe that it is. We think that the commonly
expressed scepticism on the subject is unwarranted,

and that it is due, partly to ignorance of what has already been achieved, partly to misconception of what science is and how it is applied, and partly to impatience with a new science, which is still at much the same stage at which physics, chemistry, and biology stood only so recently as within the life-time of our great-grandparents.

Those who doubt the practical utility of sociological study and sociological inferences have in mind, perhaps, only the social institutions belonging to the first three of the four classes into which, as we have explained, the subject-matter of the science may be divided. Not unnaturally they are sceptical of the practical utility for everyday life of an exploration of the origins, in animal instinct, religious emotion, or humanistic ideals, of social relations that they prefer to take for granted. But even such critics should realise that it is not out of these, but out of the vast array of social institutions of the fourth class—those deliberately devised with a view to increasing social efficiency—that an applied science of sociology might be expected to be (and indubitably is being) constructed.

We may adduce one or two examples of the use of an applied science of society in the public administration of Great Britain during the past hundred years. In the early part of the nineteenth century the business of government, whether national or local government, was honeycombed with favouritism, corruption, and barefaced peculation. This wholesale dishonesty on the part of representatives and officials has been largely swept away by the adoption of a social invention of definitely scientific character, namely, the audit—a device which is scarcely a century old. The systematic checking of the cash transactions of all public officials by a special class of independent experts has been found, in the course of no more than a couple of generations, to have an amazing influence not only upon their accuracy but also upon their honesty. It has been proved that the world can, by taking thought, so far predict and alter the future as positively to grow the habit of honesty on a large scale. Another instance is the discovery, during the past three-quarters of a century, of better methods of selecting persons for responsible or specialised work. During the eighteenth century, alike in central and in local government, nearly all positions of trust and authority were jobbed ; that is to say, they were given by those in authority to their own relatives, political supporters, or social hangers-on, however incapable or badly conducted these persons might be.   To-day this jobbery has been very nearly eliminated in the British civil service, although not yet so completely in that of our local governing bodies, by two or three simple devices.   One of these devices, applicable to nearly all first appointments of young persons, is selection by competitive examination, through a non-political board, wholly unconnected with the public authorities which are engaging new employees. Another expedient, more suited to persons of mature age, where specific attainments are indispensable, is the device of a prescribed qualification, a qualification tested by the appropriate professional organisation, again an organisation wholly unconnected with the individuals or authorities concerned. This we have adopted, in one or other form, for our doctors and nurses, civil engineers, accountants, and architects.

It is a feature of all social institutions that, in their growth and development, they manifest characteristic diseases, which become known only by prolonged observation of an experience of their operation. We then see emerging new social institutions, more or less consciously designed to counteract or remedy the injurious effects of the older ones. Thus, one of the consequences of the competition for individual gain, which marked the social institution of profit-making capitalism, was a growth of callousness in the directors and managers of industry. These men, though they were often, and perhaps usually, pious Christians, good fathers and husbands, and public-spirited citizens, were so blinded by their belief in the social advantages of unrestricted competition that they failed to realise how tyrannous was their attitude to the individual wage-earner, to whom they paid the very lowest wage that they could drive him to accept, and whom they dismissed without provision as soon as trade declined. Not for generations was it recognised that unrestricted capitalist competition inevitably resulted in hideous slums, lowered vitality, festering diseases, and mcral as well as physical degeneration of the race. To defend themselves against the employers' tyranny the wage-earners devised the new social institution of trade unionism, experimentally working its way by trial and error to a new policy of fixing standard conditions by collective instead of individual bargaining. To protect the community against the social evils resulting from competitive capitalism experiment after experiment was tried, during the whole of the nineteenth century, in factory and mines regulation, in merchant shipping Acts, in employers' liability for accidents and industrial diseases, and in the various ramifications of public health legislation. Alike in trade unionism and in the legislative regulation of industry it is now seen that these empirical experiments may be summed up in the formulation and enforcement of a national minimum of civilised life below which, in the public interest, no individual can be permitted to fall.[1]

Let us add one more instance of the advantage to be gained by the systematic study of social facts in the manner that we have described. A hundred years ago the accepted way of dealing with extreme poverty, which was called destitution, was poor-law

[1] This is not to say that the new institutions of collective bargaining and factory legislation are free from drawbacks. Indeed, more complete, and so to speak, more scientific study of the economic relations between employers and wage-earners might conceivably have led to the conclusion that what was causing the social injury was not individual bargaining (which could, with some disadvantages, be replaced by concerted national minima), but the direction of wealth-production, whether by capitalists or wage-earners, under the incentive of individual pecuniary gain, for which another form of social organisation might possibly be substituted.

relief. This relief took one of two forms, maintenance in the general mixed workhouse or a niggardly dole of unconditional outdoor relief. A century of experience has discredited both. As a result of long-continued observation, inference, and experiment by all sorts of persons, officials, and philanthropists, recorded in innumerable blue-books and some scientific treatises, there has been gradually evolved a whole series of new social institutions dealing with the problem. A veritable framework of prevention has been substituted for a framework of repression and deterrence. Instead of threatening the destitute sick person with the workhouse if he applied for relief, the public health authority has come more and more to seek him out, in order to cure him and to prevent the spread of disease. The local education authority now welcomes every poor child to school, insists that the parents send the child to school reasonably clean and adequately booted; even feeds the child if it is found to require it, and prosecutes the parents who are guilty of wilful neglect. The infant welfare centre, improving on compulsory registration, now endeavours actively to look after every birth, instructs the mother how to rear the baby, and offers periodically to examine and weigh the growing infant, so that the mother may know how it is progressing. This instruction and inspection may seem a small matter. But the statistician proves to us that during the past thirty years, since these things have been done, only half as many babies die as in the previous generation. What is even more striking is the vast alteration for the better that has been effected by these preventive services in the behaviour of the parents and the children in healthy living, in cleanliness, and even in manners.

We quite understand how unexpected the foregoing instances of applied science will seem to the average objector. He will probably not have thought of them as being derived from science at all! Even if he regards them as improvements in society comparable to the provision of aluminium or the electric light, he will not recognise them as due to the studies of the sociologist, or as products of the scientific method. Were they not put in operation by politicians on the one hand, or by unimaginative business administrators on the other, avowedly ignorant of science? Have not such institutions been successively improved by no more scientific method than that of "Trial and Error"? This, we may observe, is how practically all changes in social structure are made, but not why they come to be made. We are, of course, not suggesting that such social reforms have been proposed by professors of sociology, or advocated in treatises claiming to deal with that subject at all. But behind the Cabinet and the House of Commons, throughout the nineteenth century, behind the leaders of business in Great Britain and the United States, even before people talked much about sociology, there were patient observers of social facts, classifying what they observed and framing tentative hypotheses as to co-existences and sequences; not presuming, as a rule, to formulate "laws of nature", or to postulate theoretical deductions from any generalisations whatever, but contented merely to draw the specific inference from their studies that if such and such action were taken, such and such beneficial results would follow. It can scarcely be denied that it is the steadily increasing knowledge of social facts that has, during the past hundred years, led to one change after another in social structure. Whatever the mathematicians and the physicists may feel about it, this is, in fact, how sociology becomes increasingly an applied science.

But here we must demolish another bogey. Some objectors to sociology, and particularly some idealistic philosophers, try to make our "flesh creep with prophecies about the future tyranny of the expert, who is going to do his best to make all men uniform, like factory-made goods. This would be plausible enough if physics were the only science. But clearly a great many of the experts would have to be experts in biology, as doctors are to-day. Now one of the first things a biologist learns is that no two frogs, let alone two men, are quite alike. And if he is a geneticist, studying heredity, he is most concerned with those differences, and particularly with the odd individuals who keep cropping up when we think we have got a true-breeding population. The founder of genetics in this country, William Bateson, left a motto for his successors, . . . It was 'Treasure your exceptions'. That represents the biological point of view, whereas the engineer's point of view is 'Scrap your exceptions. . . '. To a biologist the social problem is not 'How can we get these men and women to fit into society' but 'How can we make a society into which these men and women will fit'." [1]

It should be needless to say that what Professor Haldane so well expresses as the biological standpoint is even more decidedly that of the sociologist, whose very subject-matter is human society *as it exists* in all its infinite diversity, and who, in his studies, literally revels in this diversity.

We make no exaggerated claims for sociology at its present stage. Human society, in this year of grace, 1932, is admittedly in a sorry state. Nations calling themselves civilised seem unable to avoid the periodical self-destruction of war. In the midst of plenty, millions of men, women, and children, in America as well as in Europe and Asia, perish untimely through chronic insufficiency of food. Mass unemployment in all industrialised communities accompanies the heaping up of colossal individual fortunes that make political equality a sham. But we can register, nevertheless, some social progress. The twentieth century is not, in any civilised country, as was the eighteenth; and no small part of the change is due directly to improvements in social institutions, which have been, in fact, though often unconsciously so, the outcome of the study of society. When we reflect how little had been

[1] Professor J. B. S. Haldane, in *The Listener*, 10th February 1932.

achieved, say, in 1760, by physics and chemistry in their application to non-living matter; or, say, as late as 1820, by any branch of biology in its application to the prevention and cure of disease, the sociologist has no reason to feel discouraged at the achievements made by 1932 in the application of his own much younger science to the improvement of social institutions.

Here we touch on a special difficulty in the practical application of social science. It is one thing to effect, in any community, a change in the social institution that we call law, and quite another thing to get the change manifested in a corresponding alteration in the habits and customs of the nation. "Let me write the songs of the people", suggested Fletcher of Saltoun three hundred years ago, "and I care not who makes the laws." This, however, was an over-statement of a profound truth. A change in the law, in any society civilised enough to have laws, must necessarily be a potent cause of change of habit and custom. But habits and customs alter only gradually, even on the impulse of new laws; often, indeed, only by slow and almost imperceptible degrees—like the hour-hand on a clock dial—whilst Acts of Parliament increase by visible jumps, like the hand that marks the seconds. It is easy for a nation to change its laws as soon as it chooses to do so. It is very hard for any elderly person, hard even for any adult, to change his habits. It is immeasurably more difficult to bring about a change in the habits of the whole popula-

tion. This is true even of a people in a primitive
stage, where the routine of life is relatively simple
and uniform. It is still more true of peoples in an
advanced stage, where habits have multiplied, increased in variety, and stiffened in intensity.

This does not mean either that it is impossible to
change the habits and customs of a whole nation;
or that an alteration in the law is not a useful and
effective way of bringing about an improvement.
But there are other instruments of social change
which it is essential to bring into active co-operation
with new statute law. We may summarily include
them in the term public opinion—a supremely
powerful factor in changing habits and customs;
whether at work in the family, the school, the vocation, the associations of consumers, the organisations
for religion and culture, sport and recreation, the
locality or the nation as a whole. Every influence
that helps to create or to mould public opinion—
the spread of new knowledge, the teaching in the
schools, the utterance of the popular prophets, the
newspaper, the pulpit, the theatre, the cinema, and,
last by no means least, the "wireless broadcast"—
counts either as an ally of the new statute or as an
opponent. Whether or not the law effects the change
it aims at, or remains, as we say, a "dead-letter";
and how quickly and how completely it produces
the desired result, depends upon the side on which
the weight of public opinion comes down. There
are cases in which the mere enactment of a law
has, on a given day, suddenly changed the routine

of life of the whole people — the adoption of "summer time" is a striking example. In other cases the change of life demanded by the law has not failed to occur, but it has come about only step by step, in the course of a generation—for instance, the requirement that parents should send their children to school regularly, punctually, reasonably clean, and adequately clothed. It is not easy to decide whether the establishment of representative institutions and the adoption of universal suffrage make it easier or more difficult to alter the social institutions of a nation. A dictatorship promises quicker law-making, but runs a great risk of increasing popular resistance to change. On the other hand, the discussions and delays involved in democratic institutions make it more difficult to get a new law, but greatly promote the "consciousness of consent", which causes the law to be obeyed. It may be added that, in social matters, to change simultaneously the form and the substance may be more logical, but it is also much more provocative and troublesome than taking them one at a time. It is usually easier, as well as more important, gradually to alter the substance by itself, whilst leaving the form unchanged. To change the form involves a sudden jump, which maximises opposition, whilst not necessarily at once effecting any alteration in the substance. Yet it is desirable, from time to time, to make the effort necessary to bring the old form into accord with the new substance, both for the sake of definitely ensuring the permanence of the improvement, and with the object of giving the forward movement a new start. Thus the net effect of the study of sociology is, one way or another, to make for change.

But sociology is a science with its own definite limitations. For one thing, as we have mentioned, its very subject-matter is perpetually altering in kind and quality as well as in quantity and location. Unlike iron and stone, heat and light, human beings and their social institutions are always changing. They even alter whilst we are studying them. This is a difficulty which the science of sociology shares with the science of biology, at any rate in its application to medicine or to genetics. But the mobility does not entirely prevent our forecasting of results or the practical use of social prediction in the world's affairs. The administrators of our posts and telegraphs, and those of our railway and omnibus services, find it possible to make extraordinarily accurate predictions, within quite definite limits of error, as to the number of letters and passengers to be expected on a given day. Yet whilst some of our commonest sociological predictions may be thus relatively not much further from perfect accuracy than those of the astronomers, it must be admitted that changes in social institutions are sometimes so catastrophic and far-reaching as completely to baffle our generalisations and nullify our predictions. No student, however competent, even if he could have forecast the Russian Revolution of 1917, could have predicted the nature of the

Soviet State in 1932. No one could have foreseen the sudden development in 1922 of the Fascist state in Italy. No one could have predicted at the opening of the twentieth century the rapid rise to prosperity and power of the Czecho-Slovakian Republic, the very name of which we could barely pronounce and the exact position of which was then unknown to most of us. Here and there, from time to time, there emerges from the mass a man or a group of men whose uncommon qualities are exceptionally influential with the particular race of human beings with whom they come in contact. It may be a captivating personality, it may be religious exaltation, it may be superlative efficiency in the organisation of war or in the administration of the state. Such social "ferments"—to use the phrase of William James—are influences which change the course of life of a whole nation. We may recognise such a ferment in the great leader of the Czecho-Slovakian race, Masaryk. Sometimes these potent individuals appear more like volcanic eruptions—as with Lenin in Russia and Mussolini in Italy and Gandhi in India. These are as unpredictable by science as an earthquake. But woe betide the great man, be he prophet, or warrior, or statesman, who forgets not only that the common man exists, but also that it is with the common man that he has to deal. If a Lenin, a Mussolini, or a Gandhi wants to reduce the infant death-rate, or to shorten the factory day, to create a universal system of public education or to build up a stable democratic state out of millions of men of different races and antagonistic creeds, in Russia, in Italy, or India, he must, for all his volcanic power, learn from the systematised facts of past and present social institutions, that is, from the science of sociology, the particular devices by which one or other of these things can be created.

Thus the generalisation and predictions of the science of society relate to that strange abstraction, the average human being. Here we recognise what might be termed the mystical element in the work of the statistician. What he tells us is truth, even truth of a high order. But he does not deal with our individual peculiarities. He predicts what will be found true of that which is common to all the individuals who make up the group or race of men with which he is dealing. The uncommon, the exceptional, the peculiar characteristics of the individual man, and the manner of his influence, are at present, and possibly always will be, outside the scope of a science of society.

But there is a second question which continuously confronts the open-minded devotee of science, whether in the biological or in the physical group of sciences. Is man's capacity for scientific discovery the only faculty required for the reorganisation of society according to an ideal? Or do we need religion as well as science, emotional faith as well as intellectual curiosity?

We suggest that, in all its forms and in all its achievements, science deals only with processes; it has nothing to say of the purpose, either of our own life, or of the universe. We can learn through science how best to kill a man or slaughter a multitude of men; we can discover how to cure a human being of specific diseases and thus raise indefinitely the standard of health; we can suggest the particular social institutions that will lessen human misery. But no personal observation or statistical enquiry, nor any amount of scientific knowledge, will tell us whether we *ought* to kill or to cure. Our behaviour, as parent or child, as colleague or rival, as employer or employed, as private citizen or public official, is largely dictated to us by law or public opinion. Whenever the individual settles it for himself it seems to depend ultimately on intuition or impulse, on likes or dislikes, or to put it in another way, on the emotional outlook on life. Historically speaking, codes of conduct, scales of value, or to use the term of Professor Graham Wallas, patterns of behaviour—seem always to have been intimately related to contemporary conceptions of man's relation to the universe, or of the relation of the individual to his fellow men, whether these notions are woven into magic rites, wrought into religious creeds or humanistic ideals, or expressed in systems of philosophy, all alike incapable of objective—that is to say, scientific— verification. In the world's past experience it seems as if, in what we choose to regard as the nobler type of men, these guides to conduct rise out of emotive thought, connecting an ideal of human behaviour either with some conception of the purpose of life, or with some assumed purpose of the universe itself. All that can be done is for each person to express his own state of mind, so that he may enter into communion with those of like temperament, and thus encourage and strengthen each other in the common pilgrimage through life. To many it seems that the mind of man, as distinguished from the appetites and instincts which he shares with other animals, is divided into two parts—the intellectual and the emotional, each having its own methods and sanctions. What is called the scientific method is the highest expression of the intellect; by observation, verification, and reasoning we can discover how things happen and predict how they will happen under like circumstances; and, in many instances, by applying this knowledge, we can alter this happening in the direction we desire.

On the other hand, the highest, or most desirable, expression of the emotional side of human nature is, as the world agrees to believe, either the attainment of the beautiful, or, in the alternative, the attainment of the good, or, as some would say, the holy. The quest of the beautiful is represented by every form of art. The quest of the good or the holy is represented, on the one view, by manifestations of humanistic ideals; and, on the other, by all the varieties of what must be termed—whether or not any theistic basis can be traced—religious experience. In any one of these ways, and in many combinations of them, individual men and women, all through the ages, have found in their minds indications, unknown to science, of what is the purpose of the universe, or, at least, of what should be made the object of their own lives. They have thereby discovered rules or guidance which are justified to themselves by their effect on their own emotional consciousness, and by which they can direct their own conduct, including their individual use of whatever scientific knowledge they possess. In any case it is not to the intellectual outcome of science, but to some feeling in the individual consciousness, that we must look for guidance as to how to use the powers that we possess.

We are conscious that this cold analysis of the outcome of the emotional side of human nature fails altogether to express the warmth and fervour and potency, alike of the artistic temperament or of that of humanism or religion. Those who have the artistic temperament will know in what states of consciousness this may be embodied, and what may be its guidance, its discipline, and its sanctions in the conduct of life. Those for whom art is not the highest expression of their emotional nature may, like the majority of mankind within historic times, seek mental security in a "spiritual home", to which some of them may assign a humanistic and others a religious denomination. In this fourth decade of the twentieth century some may recall how Auguste Comte, nearly a hundred years ago, declared that "our harmony as moral beings is impossible on any other foundation but altruism. Nay more, altruism alone can enable us to live in the highest and truest sense. To live for others is the only means of developing the whole existence of man. Towards Humanity, who is the only true Great Being, we, the conscious elements of whom She is the compound, shall henceforth direct every aspect of our life, individual and collective. Our thoughts will be devoted to the knowledge of Humanity, our affections to her love, our actions to her service."[1] Probably a larger number of people will prefer the glowing if less definite creed of a contemporary scientist. "Religion", we are told by Professor Whitehead,[2] "is a vision of something which stands beyond, behind, and within the passing flux of immediate things; something which is real, and yet waiting to be realised; something which is a remote possibility, and yet the greatest of present facts; something that gives meaning to all that passes, and yet eludes apprehension; something whose possession is the final good, and yet is beyond all reach; something which is the ultimate ideal, and the hopeless quest."

[1] It will seem paradoxical to many even to enquire whether something like Auguste Comte's *Religion of Humanity* may not be the spirit inspiring the extraordinary experiment of Lenin and Stalin in Soviet Russia in constructing, out of the intellectual dialectic of Karl Marx, a whole series of brand-new social institutions, pursuing them, if by nothing better than "Trial and Error", until they succeed in bringing them in conformity with an applied science of society for the advantage, as they believe, not of themselves, but of the workers of the world.

[2] *Religion and the Modern World*, by A. N. Whitehead, p. 238.

INDEX

Acton, Lord, 230
Animal instinct as origin, 23, 24
Audit, 28, 243

Bacon, Roger, 234
Baltimore City Council, 183-4
Barnes, G. N., 167
Bateson, William, 248
Bernheim, Ernst, 44, 101
Bias, invariable presence of, 44, 45
Bingham, W. V., 130
Biology, relation of sociology to, 3, 6, 10, 11
Booth, Charles, 206-10
Borough extension, enquiry into, 179-81
Boston City Council, 181-3
Bowley, A. L., 202, 205, 210, 212, 213, 214, 215, 228
Browne, Sir Thomas, 235
Bryce, Viscount, 187
Burnett-Hurst, A. R., 210
Burns, John, 162
Butler, Samuel, 65

Challenger Expedition, 8
Class, nature of, 15
Classification of the sciences, 5-14; problem of, 57-60
Clifford, F., 116
Clutton-Brock, A., 32
Cohen, Morris, 15, 34
Committee government in U.S.A., 185-6
Commons, John R., 2
Comte, Auguste, 238, 259
Cooley, C. H., 18, 64

Cox, J., 235
Cox, J. C., 55
Curie, Madam, 238

Diary, extracts from, 160-187, 194-8
Documents, definition of, 100; use of, 104-11; application of sampling to, 112-17

Edgeworth, F. Y., 217
Edison, T. A., 33, 67
Efficiency as object, 28, 29
Ehrlich, 67
Einstein, 33
Engineers, Amalgamated Society of, 161-7
Experiment, how far practicable in sociology, 220-26

Faraday, M., 67
Fees charged to researchers, 106
Five-Year Plan, 29

Galton, F. W., 162
Gandhi, 254
George, H. B., 102
Glasgow, trade unionism in, 189-93
Goethe, W. von, 48
Gooch, G. P., 99
Gurney, W. S., 122
Guyot-Daubés, 84

Haldane, J. B. S., 34, 65, 66, 219, 248, 249
Haldane, Viscount, 150
Halévy, Élie, 229
Hall, Hubert, 102, 105

Harvey, William, 235
Hayes, E. L., 20, 21
Hazlitt, William, 48
Hegel, 14
Heraclitus, 34
Hobhouse, L. T., 16, 17
Hobson, J. A., 45
Hogg, M. H., 210
Humanistic ideals as origin, 26, 27
Hypothesis, use of, 43, 60, 61; need for more than one, 61; advantage of a collection, 61-2; how to evolve, 63-6

Institutions, definitions of, 2; suggested classifications of, 22-30
Interview, the Method of the, 130, 131, 135-41

James, William, 5, 57, 254

Kultur, 4

Langlois, Charles, and Seignobos, Charles, 50, 99, 231
Larmor, Sir J., 65
Law of Diminishing Returns in sociology, 231
Lenin, 254
Leonardo da Vinci, 235
Literature, use of, in research, 117-129
Little, W. C., 148
Local Acts, 107, 115-17
Locke, John, 12
Lowell, Lawrence, 229
Lysons, D., 122

Maciver, R. R., 2, 11
Mackinder, Sir Halford, 5, 7
Mainwaring, 119, 121
Maitland, F. W., 115
Maitland, W., 122
Manchester City Council, 194-8
Mann, Tom, 162
Marx, Karl, 14, 39
Masaryk, 254
Materialist conception of history, 14

Mendel, 236
Mental equipment required, 31-53
Merceron, Joseph, 119-23
Miners' Federation, 167-78
Moore, B. V., 130
Mussolini, 254

Newton, Sir Isaac, 33, 235
Notes, specimen, 97
Note-taking, the art of, 83-97; form and method of notes, 84-8; the use of shuffling the pack of notes, 90-96; an instrument of discovery, 93-6

Open mind, what it is, 46
Oral evidence, use and misuse of, 143-56

Parliament, 19, 20
Pestalozzi, 12
Philadelphia City Council, 184-5
Poincaré, Henri, 9, 65
Politsphere, 8
Predictions seldom quite accurate, even in astronomy, 227
Psychology, relation of sociology to, 11, 12
Publication, 234-40; required for complete verification, 236; methods of, 237-40
Purpose of life, relation of sociology to the, 241-59; given by religious emotion, 256-9; science bankrupt of purpose, 255-6

Questionnaire, use and misuse of the, 68-82; injurious effects of the, 70-73; examples of the, 73-82

Ramsay, Sir W., 227, 239
Ranke, 99
Rayleigh, Lord, 227, 239
Religious emotion as origin, 25; as determining purpose, 256; as source of scale of values, 256-9
Rhodes, Thomas, 123
Rickert, Heinrich, 12
Rousseau, J. J., 12, 13

Royal Commissions, advantages and defects of, 142-57; various methods used by, 143-50; Lord Beaconsfield on, 143

Russia, Soviet, 14, 15, 27, 224, 254-5, 259

Sampling, method of, 210-12
Schaeffle, Albert, 238
Schumpeter, Josef, 45, 111, 137, 233
Scientific management, 29
Shakespeare, William, 48
Shaw, Bernard, 102
Sidgwick, Henry, 238
Simon, Sir Ernest, 198
Social facts, what they are, 54, 55; how they can be studied, 54-82
Sociology, province of, 1-30; origin of word, 1; subject-matter of, 3-12; belonging to biological group, 3; relation to psychology, 11, 12
Sociology, applied, nature and progress of, 242-8
Sociosphere, 8
Spencer, F. H., 116
Spencer, Herbert, 12, 36

Spoken Word, the, 130-41
Spry, W. J. J., 8
Statistics, use of, in sociological research, 202-17; conditions on which its value depends, 203-6; limitations of use of, in discovery, 215-17
Steffens, Lincoln, 199
Summer Time, 28

Thompson, Sir C. W., 8

Verification, 218-33

Wallas, Graham, 62, 63, 65, 159, 218, 256
Ward, Lester F., 1, 2, 24, 57
Watching the Institution at work, 158-201
Waterston, 236
Weber, Max, 12
Wells, H. G., 10
Whewell, W., 15, 57, 58, 59
Whitehead, E. N., 259
Wilson, T. Woodrow, 187
Wolf, A., 58, 60, 62
Written Word, the, 98-129; classification of, 99-101

THE END